Loyalty, Intensity, and Passion

An inside look at the National Lacrosse League

by

Debbie Elicksen

Also by Debbie Elicksen

Future Prospects, *ISBN 978-09730237-4-9*
Sports, 2005, Softcover, $15
5.25" x 8.25" – 118 pages
18 black and white photos
Rights held: world, English,
www.freelancepublishing.net

Inside the NHL Dream, *ISBN 978-09730237-0-1*
Sports, 2002, Softcover, $15
5.25" x 8.25" – 192 pages
13 black and white photos
Rights held: world, English,
www.freelancepublishing.net

Positive Sports, *ISBN 978-09730237-3-2*
Sports, 2003, Softcover, $15
5.5" x 8.5" – 144 pages
17 black and white photos
Rights held: world, English,
www.freelancepublishing.net

Self-Publishing 101, *ISBN 978-1-55180-639-6*
Publishing, 2005, Softcover
8.25" x 9.75" – 174 pages
Rights held: world, English
Self-Counsel Press, www.self-counsel.com

Calgary Booster Club: Creating a Legacy
ISBN 978-09730237-2-5
Sports, 2003, Softcover Not available
5.5" x 8.5" – 144 pages
17 black and white photos
Rights held: world, English,
www.freelancepublishing.net, Calgary Booster Club

What they're saying about books by Debbie Elicksen

"Despite the burgeoning success of professional indoor lacrosse, few reporters – with one or two notable exceptions – understand the game well enough to write about it with excellence or insight. Deb Elicksen is among those few scribes who through their writing demand respect from players, management and fans alike. She knows boxla because she passionately follows the National Lacrosse League (mostly through the ups and downs of the Calgary Roughnecks); has the moxie to go into the locker room after games to talk to players, even when they've lost a home playoff game, and the common sense and social wherewithal to meet and mix with the athletes away from the arena. In short, Elicksen knows the NLL inside and out. Not surprisingly therefore, "Loyalty, Intensity and Passion" is a must read for those who love the fastest game in the world played on two feet." **Bob Poole, Calgary Roughnecks**, 2005 NLL Public Relations Executive of the Year

"It was endlessly fascinating." **Vicki Gabereau** about Inside the NHL Dream

"I really like this book and one of the reasons why is she touches on all aspects of the pro game. She talks about a lot of the great players in the game—coaches, management, all these people and talks about all the different elements. I thought it was really cool. James Patrick was terrific. He talked about the commitment that may be (some players) should listen to or read this book." **Kelly Hrudey** about Inside the NHL Dream

"What a great book! I picked it up at my local Borders store in Michigan about a week ago, and I have been reading and re re-reading it since. I think this is one of the best books about hockey I have ever read." Mark from Flint, Michigan about Inside the NHL Dream

"I would just like to say that it was a fantastic book. Playing in the NHL is a dream of mine so to learn about the business part of the game and what goes on behind the scenes was of great interest to me. I love hockey and I love learning about it. I really enjoyed this book from start to finish." Bryce from Houghton, Michigan about Inside the NHL Dream

"As a player-agent, I particularly enjoyed Chapter 4—The Agent's Role, and I enjoyed your style of writing." **Bobby Orr** about Inside the NHL Dream

"A must read - tells it like it is. Thorough, thoughtful, insightful. More than a peek - a long penetrating stare at contemporary hockey's grassroots and underpinnings, superbly presented." **Art Breeze,** Pro-REP Entertainment Group about Inside the NHL Dream

"You told it like it is. The NHL is full of great athletes that have paid the price, appreciate it and give it back. Everyone we see, players we meet, I am very grateful that I have been given the chance to allow my son to meet young men from other countries by way of the NHL and by reading books like yours, showing him that, no matter what you want to do in the future, it takes hard work." Michael from Land O Lakes, Florida about Inside the NHL Dream

"When I picked your book up on Saturday morning I had absolutely no intention of reading it cover to cover in one sitting. The telephone was ringing and e-mails were piling up as is usual in my life. Still, I was so entranced with the player commentary that I could not put the book down. Next time I am at a hockey game I will most certainly view every aspect of the game in a different light because of your book." Richard from Montreal about Inside the NHL Dream

"I want to thank you for taking the time for writing a book that is long overdue. Thank you from all hockey fans." Barbara from Albuquerque, New Mexico about Inside the NHL Dream

"Many, many thanks for the book – I certainly enjoyed reading it!" **Lou Lamoriello** about Inside the NHL Dream

"Thank you for an amazing book. The overall contents is pretty inspiring. I feel the book gives the reader a good sights on what it takes in order to succeed, devotion, time, and sacrifices. Terrific writing, interesting topics all the way through." Simon from Sweden about Inside the NHL Dream

"I just read your book; it was great. A must read for all aspiring players, coaches, and trainers." Ed from Vancouver, B.C. about Inside the NHL Dream

"I just finished reading your book titled Self-Publishing 101. You did a wonderful job clearing up some of the clutter for those of us who are thinking about self-publishing. Thank you!" Dorraine about Self-Publishing 101

"This is my kind of book. It's concise, yet packed with valuable information and practical, contemporary samples. This one pulled everything together for me and suddenly it didn't seem so overwhelming. I found it to be particularly valuable in the marketing stage." Yvonne on Self-Publishing 101

"The book provides solid content, organization to die for, a brutally honest approach, a fast-paced style, and lots of helpful extras. It provides both encouragement and a healthy measure of reality to a writer considering publishing a manuscript." Janet Arnett, Canadian Book Review Annual, March/April 2007 on Self-Publishing 101

"I love it…it is very informative. I have learned a lot." Brian from Franklin, Ohio on Self-Publishing 101

"I recommended your book to a group of writers attending my Insiders Guide to Getting Published" workshop I held here at Humber last week. And it's on the recommended reading list for my program." **Cynthia Good**, Program Director, The Creative Book Publishing Program, School for Creative & Performing Arts on Self-Publishing 101

"I just finished your book, Self Publishing 101, and thought it was fantastic!" Nicole on Self-Publishing 101

Loyalty, Intensity, and Passion

An inside look at the National Lacrosse League

Freelance Communications
Calgary, Alberta
www.freelancepublishing.net

by

Debbie Elicksen

Library and Archives Canada Cataloguing in Publication

Elicksen, Debbie
        Loyalty, Intensity, and Passion: an inside look at the
National Lacrosse League / Debbie Elicksen.--First Edition

Includes bibliographical references.
ISBN 978-0-9730237-5-6

1. Lacrosse--Canada. 2. Lacrosse--United States. 3. National
Lacrosse League I. Title.

GV989.E452007   796.34'7   C2007-904015-2

Publisher
Freelance Communications
Calgary, Alberta, Canada
www.freelancepublishing.net

Design and Production
Nadien Cole Advertising

Photography:
Action Shots - Cory Shannon, email: corephoto@shaw.ca
Other - Debbie Elicksen
Back cover - Mitch Redshaw

Printing
Transcontinental, Sherbrooke, Quebec

Loyalty, Intensity, and Passion – First Edition
Printed and Bound in Canada
Copyright 2007

DEDICATION

To Tracey Kelusky, Kaleb Toth, Casey Powell,
Jim Moss, Bob Poole, Mitch Redshaw, Kurt Silcott,
and all the wonderful people I've met through lacrosse.

ACKNOWLEDGEMENTS

The following people were instrumental in providing me with the text for this book by their generous offering of time:

A special thank you to Mitch Redshaw, Bob Poole, Lisa Hoffart, Tracey Kelusky, Kaleb Toth, Jim Moss, Casey Powell, Scott Smith, Anthony Cosmo, Lewis Ratcliff, Luke Gilbert, Brad MacDonald, Brad Banister, Damien Davis, Brad Berrow, Taylor Wray, Kyle Goundrey, Kevin Dostie, John Tavares, John Grant Sr., Pat McCready, Jamey Bowen, Kurt Silcott, Chris Hall, Andy Ogilvie, Devan Wray, Jim Jennings, and Kyle Neufeld.

It's impossible to embark on such an undertaking without the kind words of support from colleagues and friends: Donna Matheson, Audrey Bakewell, Don and Molly Henderson, Arnie Jackson, Janice Delude, Pamela and Daniel Clark, Dave Rowe, Pat Clayton, Stan Schwartz, Donna Armstrong, Peter Watts, Sharon Eberson, Nadien Cole, Art Breeze, Bobbie-Jo Bergner, Darren Friesen, Laurence Heinen, Ty Pilson, Cory Shannon, John Down, Mark Stephen, Radio 27 Bob MacGillivray, Billie Rae and Ian Busby, Al Tate, Keith and Carol Evans, Doug Rooke, Stan Fischler, and especially, Lisa Hoffart and the Calgary Roughnecks.

TABLE OF CONTENTS

INTRODUCTION 12

PART ONE: PIONEERS 15
    Chapter One: History of Professional Lacrosse 16
    Chapter Two: Pioneering the Future 23

PART TWO: THE GAME 37
    Chapter Three: The Game 38
    Chapter Four: Factoring Elements 47
        League Rules 47
        On the Floor.. 49

PART THREE: THE BUSINESS 53
    Chapter Five: Contracts and Agents 54
    Chapter Six: Team Dynamics................................... 60

PART FOUR: THE PLAYERS 71
    Chapter Seven: Commitment 81
        The Money 83
        Playing With Pain 84
        Longevity 93
    Chapter Eight: Canada Versus U.S. 97

PART FIVE: LACROSSE ONE STEP FARTHER ············· 103
    Chapter Nine: Other Cups and Tournaments··············· 104
        Mann Cup ·· 104
        Minto Cup ·· 106
        Other Trophies and Cups ······························· 106
        College ·· 107
        International ·· 109
    Chapter Ten: Growth and Development ··················· 115
        Grassroots ··· 115
        Growth of the Game ···································· 122
    Chapter Eleven: Conclusion – For the Love of the Game 127

BIBLIOGRAPHY 136

ABOUT THE AUTHOR 138

INTRODUCTION

Calgary Roughnecks Director of Lacrosse Operations Mitch Redshaw relentlessly hounded me because he knew my business was writing and producing books. He nagged and nagged me until I finally succumbed. Do a book on lacrosse.

I have to admit, I didn't know very much about the game at first. Yes, I knew the rules and had even witnessed some lacrosse in Edmonton, including the Commonwealth Games, but the National Lacrosse League was foreign to me.

Then a funny thing happened at the rink (Pengrowth Saddledome in Calgary). After one encounter – just one – I was hooked. I wanted to find out from the players what made this game tick. Why does it only take one game to lure a new fan? Thus the journey to penning this book began.

What drew me closer to the game were the players. They were amazingly approachable and refreshingly cooperative in actually wanting to talk to media to help promote their game. In fact, everyone around the game is great to work with. I met very few egos in this league.

Then I got even closer. So close, in fact, that now my right of passage into every professional sports dressing room, not just lacrosse, is a five-inch surgical scar smack dab in the middle of my right knee. I was tapped on the shoulder by 2005's Curse of the Roughnecks.

"In lacrosse, you don't get a lot of knee injuries," reflects Roughneck's forward Kaleb Toth. "It's more bumps and bruises. Every time you're on the floor, you're getting bumped around, pushed, and whacked. The biggest injury guys get is turf burn or scrapes on their knees and arms."

That said, then the 2005 Calgary Roughnecks were an anomaly.

In fact, this is a team that had so many knee injuries – serious knee injuries – that the players were calling it The Curse of the Roughnecks.

Ryan McNish (defense), Andy Ogilvie (defense), Devan Wray (transition), and Matt Green (offense) were lost to the 2005 season, but that's not all. Bad knee karma also affected Jesse Phillips (defense). Transition Kyle Neufeld finally suited up in 2006 for his first NLL game thanks to his knee injury.

So imagine the scare when the club's star captain forward Tracey Kelusky woke up one morning to discover a bit of a knee problem himself. "I have no idea where I picked it up," he said. "All I know is I awoke, and my knee was four times its usual size." A couple of anti-inflammatories and he was back in the lineup. Not so for everyone else.

My experience with The Curse happened at a media shootaround session with the Calgary team the day before their playoff game against Arizona. I was going in to take a fancy backhand shot at goalie Curtis Palidwor, (using a clever move I was taught in an earlier drill) and just as I released the ball, my right leg turned to Jell-O. I did a face plant into the turf. The team immediately recognized The Curse. A torn ACL; cure: reconstruction.

There was lots of friendly advice. Andy Ogilvie is a knee expert, having had five knee surgeries. I didn't feel so bad after talking to him. Then Kyle Neufeld scared the heck out of me. Actually, they both did. I thought for sure I was going to be bedridden for a week after surgery, maybe even two. Fortunately, that wasn't the case. I survived and managed through The Curse.

Roughnecks' trainer Lisa Hoffart coached me through rehab, although, she may be the last person the players and I want to see for any "TLC" treatment. I'm sure my hand impressions are still on the Canadian Sport Rehabilitation Clinic bed after the leg massage I received from her.

Aside from the knee bonding, I came to the conclusion that the National Lacrosse League is something every sports fan needs to experience to appreciate. Just watch one game. It's exciting, fast-paced, rough with a sprinkling of finesse, and if you like to rock, the music is great.

So Mitch, you can stop bugging me now.

PART ONE
PIONEERS

"We also are men of like passions with you."
Acts of the Apostles 12:15
The Bible (Unauthorized Version, 1611)

Chapter One:

History of Professional Lacrosse

"The natural man has only two primal passions,
to get and beget."
Arthur O'Shaughnessy

Lacrosse is a game that transcends economic background, race, and occupation. The loyalty, intensity, and passion stem right back to when it was first played by Native Americans. Lacrosse was considered a gift from God. Games were part of religious holidays and scheduled to accompany the change of seasons or the position of the heavenly bodies.

Losses always weigh heavily upon an athlete's shoulders but during these times, players considered them offensive to the Holy Spirit. Mandatory ritual cleansing before and after games kept the game's pureness in tact.

There was no standardized ball size, rawhide or deerskin cover, and the New England Iroquois used a stick that has since been adapted to today's game. Of course, there was no such thing as helmets, either. The uniform mainly consisted of a loin cloth – an interesting concept in translating for today's environment.

Lacrosse was first discovered by the outside world in the 1600s when Europeans traveling to the New World witnessed these natives playing the unique ball game.

Ill health plagued Jesuit missionary Jean de Brebeuf (1593-1649) after he entered the Jesuit novitiate at Rouen before he ventured to Canada. He worked to convert the Indians to Christianity and became an astute observer, learning their culture and language. He helped other Jesuit missionaries relate to the Hurons by drawing up a list of instructions as to how to connect.

He watched the Hurons engage in the sport and reported it to his superiors in France. When de Brebeuf relayed his observations of the game of lacrosse, he didn't allude to how the game was played, but he gave it the name Ala crosse. The sticks the Hurons used reminded him of the Bishop's crozier or Acrosse, a staff carried in religious ceremonies that represented the church.

The Indians were using a rubber ball that was eight inches in diameter and weighed approximately five ounces. A Montreal dentist by the name of Dr. George Beers, who later became the "Father of Lacrosse," replaced it with a hard rubber ball.

He formed the Montreal Lacrosse Club in 1856 and published the game's first book: "Lacrosse: The National Game of Canada." Beers also created the game's first set of rules in 1867 when he formed the Canadian National Lacrosse Association. It was a major step to modernizing the game.

That same year, lacrosse was introduced to the United States when Canadian Indians demonstrated the sport at the New York Sarasota Springs fairgrounds. Soon after, eight Canadian Indians and eight Americans played an exhibition game in Troy, New York, which in turn spawned the first U.S. lacrosse club: Mohawk Club of Troy.

The new game spread quickly. The English Lacrosse Association was formed in 1868. In 1874, it was introduced to Australia. The game also grew interest in England, Ireland, France, New Zealand, and Scotland.

Intercollegiate lacrosse was born in New York City in 1877 when New York University played Manhattan College.

John R. Flannery promoted the game so heavily in the Boston and New York areas that he was soon called the father of American lacrosse, although it was his doctor's son, William H. Maddren, whom he impressed the most. Maddren played while he attended Brooklyn Polytechnic in 1892 and did graduate work at John Hopkins University, where he received an M.D. He loved lacrosse so much, he tirelessly promoted the sport throughout the Baltimore area.

Flannery formed the United States National Amateur Lacrosse Association in 1879. Its membership included 11 college and club teams. The league eventually brought about the first intercollegiate lacrosse tournament in 1881.

In 1882, the Intercollegiate Lacrosse Association was formed. The Crescent Athletic Club was created in 1894, which later became the catalyst for U.S. lacrosse development as the team dominated the game for 40-some years.

John Hopkins' associates called William C. Schmeisser "Father Bill." The lacrosse team captain turned to coaching after his intercollegiate playing career expired. He published the first standard instructional manual in

1904. "Lacrosse: From Candidate to Team" was a 113-page textbook for coaching lacrosse. Schmeisser introduced lacrosse to many schools, colleges, and even the U.S. Naval Academy. He went to the Amsterdam Olympic Games in 1928 representing the U.S. A lawyer by trade, Schmeisser served the lacrosse community exclusively as a labor of love.

The. U.S. Intercollegiate Lacrosse League was founded in 1905, and in 1907, the U.S. Military Academy played its first game. The U.S. Intercollegiate Lacrosse Association replaced the USILL in 1926.

Lacrosse had been known as Canada's national game since 1859. But when the country adopted box lacrosse, that marked a separation with the U.S., as the Americans preferred field.

The Lacrosse Hall of Fame Foundation founded a non-profit organization for the support and development of American lacrosse in 1959. It later became known as Lacrosse Foundation, and now U.S. Lacrosse.

The sport continued to grow. Club lacrosse peaked in the 1970s, and in 1971, the first NCAA lacrosse championship tournament was held. The 1978 World Series of Lacrosse was brought to Manchester, England. The Lacrosse Foundation and Baltimore's Masonic Boumi Temple sponsored Lacrosse International in 1983, where 400 players participated at all levels and were watched by 17,000 fans.

There have been a handful of professional leagues come and go after the turn of the century. In 1931, box lacrosse went pro with the Canadian Professional Indoor

Lacrosse League. It was formed with four teams: Montreal Canadiens, Montreal Maroons, Toronto Maple Leafs, and Cornwall Colts, however it closed shop the following year.

The National Lacrosse Association was formed in 1968 with the Montreal Canadiens, Toronto Maple Leafs, Detroit Olympics, Peterborough Lakers, Vancouver Carlings, Victoria Shamrocks, New Westminster Salmonbellies, and Portland (Oregon) Adanacs. It also introduced the 30-second shot clock. Again, the league folded in 1969.

A four-team Eastern Professional Lacrosse League operated for one season in 1969.

The first National Lacrosse League operated for two seasons (1974 and 1975). Its franchises included Baltimore,

Photo by Cory Shannon

Boston, Long Island, Montreal, Philadelphia, Quebec, Rochester, Syracuse, and Toronto.

The Eagle Pro Box Lacrosse League was launched in 1987 with four teams and a six-game schedule. Russ Cline and Chris Fritz were co-founders. Fritz served as President and Cline as Executive Vice President.

The league became known as the Major Indoor Lacrosse League (MILL) in 1988. It expanded to six teams and eight games in that same year.

The MILL became the National Lacrosse League in 1997, and in 1998, it abandoned its single-entity ownership strategy where teams were operated by the league.

"Founders Chris Fritz and Russ Klein currently still own the Philadelphia team," reports NLL Commissioner Jim Jennings. "They started the league and ran it from 1987 to 1997. But it was more of a single entity league. They kind of just did shows. They really didn't have a set function. They just kind of took a tractor-trailer and went to different arenas to showcase the sport. In 1997, the league changed to the NLL. We got more legitimate owners and put in more of a structure. That's really how the league began."

Today, most teams are owned and operated by the National Hockey League and National Basketball teams in their respective markets and play in the same arenas. But Cline and Fritz did influence the way the game has been presented and promoted.

The NLL features the best lacrosse players in the world and with teams in Canada and the United States, the league has continued to expand. Starting in 2008, Boston will become the league's 14th franchise. Other teams are Arizona Sting, Buffalo Bandits, Calgary Roughnecks, Chicago Shamrox, Colorado Mammoth, Edmonton Rush, Minnesota Swarm, New York Titans, Portland LumberJax, Philadelphia Wings, Rochester Knighthawks, San Jose Stealth, and Toronto Rock.

Teams play a 16-game schedule (eight home and away) and bide for the opportunity to win the Champion's Cup. Most games are played on the weekend, although some are held on weekdays.

Add to the mix a professional outdoor field. In 2001, the Major League Lacrosse was born with six U.S. franchises.

An inherent component of heritage and spiritual culture still permeates the game of lacrosse. It is considered the leading indigenous game in North America. However, its reach stretches the globe, with loyal advocates in 20 nations worldwide. Besides Canada and the U.S., these nations include Australia, Czech Republic, England, Germany, Ireland, Iroquois Nation, Japan, Korea, New Zealand, Scotland, Sweden, Wales, Argentina, Denmark, Hong Kong, Finland, Italy, and Tonga.

The respect for the game is landmark with a long family history of players breaching decades of generations.

Pat McCready: "We were bussing down to Philadelphia after a night of partying. A guy, who will remain nameless, had dentures from playing the game. In lacrosse, you get high-sticked and stuff, so he lost his teeth. He ended up going to the bathroom. In the process of getting sick in the back of the bus, his dentures fell out. Needless to say, he didn't have a dental plan, and they were worth about $1,500. He tried to go through where everything goes and ended up being sick a couple more times. At which point, the bus driver steps in, gets the teeth out. Believe it or not, the guy went and washed his teeth off. When he came back on the bus wearing his teeth, they were blue from the dye in the water."

Chapter Two:

Pioneering the Future

"Passion, I see, is catching."
William Shakespeare
Julius Caesar (1599) Act 3, Scene 1

In looking at the National Hockey League and its pioneers, the Bobby Orrs and the Gordie Howes who helped promote the game of hockey and brought it to a whole new level, factoring in how little money they made compared to today's standards – it's easy to try and compare the National Lacrosse League in its present form. The NLL could very well be on the cusp of a new dimension – one that will take it to new heights with network television contracts, expansion, and enough dollars to pay their players a comfortable salary.

United States-born forward Casey Powell exudes character and success everywhere he turns. He and his brother Ryan starred with Syracuse University. His NLL career has led him to Rochester, Long Island, and Anaheim. He was a two-time NCAA Player of the Year (1997, 1998), two-time Attackman of the Year (1997, 1998), Syracuse University all-time leading scorer in 2001 and 2002, three-time All-American, an NCAA champion, world champion, and an Major Lacrosse League champion. Powell and his brother Ryan own Powell Brother's Lacrosse Camps. He travels to charity and community events, promoting lacrosse at every chance he can get. He writes for E-Lacrosse and has a

SIRIUS Satellite Radio show called Inside the National Lacrosse League.

Powell was first overall in the 1998 NLL Entry Draft by Rochester. Currently a member of the New York Titans, Powell is also a first-team all star with the Rochester Rattlers of the Major League Lacrosse (MLL). He truly exemplifies the spirit and passion of the current lacrosse player.

"It's really, really hard work, flying across the country, showing up, getting your butts kicked for two and a half hours, and having to stay in shape. It's really, really hard. We're paving the way for the future of the game and hopefully making things more comfortable. The pay is getting better. More guys are living in the area where they play. The more revenue that comes in, the more players will be able to just play. It will help the sport grow, help the teams practice, and the play will be a lot better."

One could say that lacrosse is on the same cusp where women's hockey was at the time of the 2000 Olympic Winter Games in Nagano. Calgary Roughneck's president and owner Brad Banister, who started the team in 2001, thinks lacrosse is actually a little bit ahead.

"Unfortunately, the Canadian scholarships (for lacrosse) aren't here. We lose a lot of great athletes. The opportunities for lacrosse are still in the U.S."

Banister sold Blizzard Communications, a company renting satellite phones to drilling operations, to fund the NLL franchise fee, which was $500,000. He started Whitefox Environmental Services at the same time (which supplies cleanup services to the energy sector), then sold it to Peak Energy Services Ltd. in 2003. He still runs the division while moonlighting with the Roughnecks. It takes about $30,000 a week to pay the bills, of which part of that goes to their facility landlord: the Calgary Flames. Banister spent his first season also rolling out the green playing carpet at the Pengrowth Saddledome, among his many other duties.

John Grant Sr., whose son John currently plays in the NLL, pioneered during the 1970s. He has also been a childhood hero to one of the NLL's biggest stars: Tracey Kelusky. Grant grew up in Peterborough and spent two years in Philadelphia in 1974 and 1975. He was on the Canadian field lacrosse team in three World Championships, coached in the Canada Summer Games in New Brunswick, and dabbled in a number of areas of the game. Unfortunately, Grant Sr.'s professional league days were numbered.

"In 1975, Montreal and Quebec City played in the finals. It was a great rivalry. They had sellouts, even with the transit strike in Montreal. It was a great series, which Quebec ended up winning. In 1976, our owner decided not to go on with the league. He ended up buying the 76ers in Philadelphia (National Basketball Association). Problems arose with the Olympics in Montreal, where they would have had to be on the road for the first month. If they were going to have home games, they were going to have to play out of the Rocket Richard Arena. There was a power struggle in Montreal. Rochester went to Long Island. Syracuse went to Quebec City. There were some issues the first year. Maryland and Philly owners put money in to keep the Boston franchise going. It wasn't good at the top. There weren't the right people behind it. In February, it folded."

Grant Sr. knows how important getting network television means to the growth of the sport. They had tried to get their games on TSN. A 1973 one-game series for the Mann Cup was televised by CBC but it was an isolated situation. The potential for a growing television audience isn't always dependent on existing lacrosse fans.

"When you flick on a sport like lacrosse, people weren't knowledgeable about the game unless you played it. In talking to people at TSN, you can't look at the 10,000/20,000 people who know about the game. It's the other people that flick through the channels. What holds them to that time slot or that few five seconds? When you hear Joe Bowen's voice (known as the voice of the Toronto Maple Leafs and who coined the phrase "Holy Mackinaw!") when he was doing the Sportsnet games, the credibility he gave the sport – people recognized his voice from Leafs broadcasts – you might spend a little extra time. He added that charisma and excitement. It was just like listening to the Leafs play, other than it was lacrosse."

But more than television, cross-promotions also sell the game. Grant Sr. recalls how it was used to help sell a game in the 1970s.

"When the Phillies would get rained out, they would announce that the lacrosse game was available to watch. Of course, Veterans' Stadium was right across the street from the Spectrum. They would do a ticket rate. People would come over from the baseball and take in the game. It happened that the wives and girlfriends were in this section, and in comes these 15 guys. They obviously had a few pints. They're asking questions as the game is going on. They were negative at first, then all of a sudden, if you watch enough lacrosse, the end to end play, the goalie makes the save, and the transition part of the game – this was one of the games that went into overtime – these people, now after watching it, they're jumping out of their seats. They're heading to the box office to buy the remainder of the season tickets.

"The people that know the game understand it and love it. In the pro league in 1974, we played on wooden floors. The sound carried, like basketball. The running of the floor added to the game. Now with the carpet, it looks good, but it's quiet. When we went to carpet in the second year in 1975, because of man-hours, a lot of people complained. They kept saying there was something wrong with the game. They can't hear it."

One of the biggest aspects of pioneering the growth of the game comes from the professional players themselves – after the game is over.

In John Grant Sr.'s day, they connected with fans by mail.

"We'd have our own mail at the Spectrum. You'd receive letters all the time from fans. They want you to do this or that. You accommodate some of them, then you'd get a letter back – you made my son's day. Thirty years later, these guys are even more approachable."

What Grant means is today's professional player is up front and personal with their fans. It's a part of the NLL policy they strongly believe will carry the game into the future.

Kaleb Toth has played in every Calgary Roughneck game since the team's inception in the 2001-02 season. Calgary Sun sportswriter Ian Busby described Toth in a November 2001 FFWD magazine article as being to the Roughnecks what Wayne Gretzky was to the Los Angeles Kings. "A recognizable face, a tireless promoter, and a star player."

Toth started out with the Toronto Rock where he scored the game-winning goal for Toronto in the league championship game at home in 2000. The score was tied 13-13 when he made his move with 1.1 seconds left on the clock. That goal gave the Rock its second straight title.

"Off the floor, participating with the fans, you get to sign autographs and put smiles on kids' faces. A lot of professional sports don't do that kind of stuff, but we pride ourselves on being a fan-related sport. Every team has autograph sessions after the game. Every team has a post-game party, where the fans can go meet the players. That's what's going to sell our sport. We're not prima donnas or million dollar guys. We're real people that work nine to five jobs and play a sport because we love it."

Toth understands that if the game gets big enough, there will have to be some controls, but he strongly believes they will always recognize the fans.

"I think we always will, even if we start getting paid millions of dollars. After a game when you lose, you don't want to talk to anybody or sign anything, but as soon as you see a kid on the floor and he smiles at you, it kind of makes everything go away."

At the post game party, regardless of what city it takes place in, both teams participate. It also helps bring opposing players closer together.

"In lacrosse, we keep everything on the floor," adds Toth. "If there's something that goes on during the game, upstairs at the after party, everyone is friends. Everyone talks. It doesn't matter how much you dislike a player, everything gets settled on the floor. After the game, we all have the same goal in mind. Everyone is trying to grow the sport."

It doesn't matter what era or what level, the game of lacrosse seems to get inside a player's blood. A lot of people build their lives around lacrosse.

Former goalie and NLL scout Brad Berrow explains, "I left the game, and it drove me crazy. New wife, new career, then a move to Calgary. I drove to Calgary, and I thought I could see all these lacrosse boxes. I thought great. A couple days later, I'm there, streaming (to the rink) to go play. I show up, and it's a grass floor, just for hockey."

Kurt Silcott grew up in Mt. Kisco, New York. His brother Brian had switched from baseball to lacrosse, and when Kurt saw how much fun he was having, he switched, too.

He took a job with the Buffalo Sabres in 1994, initially selling tickets. Getting involved in lacrosse wasn't really on his mind as the NHL team kept him busy. But when the Sabres moved into a new arena, more opportunities presented itself, and one of the jobs that opened up was in lacrosse. Buffalo owned its own team and needed someone to run the operation.

"I think the game right now is on the cusp. It's very close to big things. We need to expose this game to more people. TV will help with that, but you come down to the rink and sit and watch lacrosse, everyone leaves entertained, and everyone loves it. It's one of those sports that the first time you're there, you can fall in love with it. Most cities have this fan base that is so passionate. There just isn't that many of them yet. That's our challenge as a league and as individual teams – to get more people out to the games to see our sport. As that happens and we continue to get into more cities, we'll continue to grow. I don't expect it to happen overnight. I think sometimes we all fall prey to try and rush it a little bit."

Silcott is currently the general manager and vice president of the Calgary Roughnecks and sees that most franchises are doing well.

"Different organizations are run different ways. In Buffalo, I was really the only full-time person dedicated to lacrosse. There were other people in the organization, such as sales and marketing people, who worked for the Sabres. They also did the Bandits. They had dual roles, but their primary role was the Sabres. In Calgary, it's different. There are people here who are all full-time staffers for the Roughnecks. In other cities, they have different versions of the same type of thing. I think the most important thing is to have a healthy relationship with the building you're playing in. Ultimately, that's the thing that's going to drive your team."

Television is certainly a key component for growing the sport. A landmark announcement was made in January 2005. NBC President Ken Schanzer and NLL

Commissioner Jim Jennings set the tone for live network TV. With the ink on the contract still fresh, the February 2005 NLL All Star Game in Calgary attracted an audience of 0.8, meaning 800,000 watched with very little prompting from lead-up advertising.

Tracey Kelusky is one of those clutch players that seem to always come through when you need it the most – especially in the last three minutes of a game. He was drafted first overall by the Columbus Landsharks. He was the NLL's 2001 Rookie of the Year, Inside Lacrosse magazine's NLL Most Valuable Player, won a gold medal with Canada at 2004 World Field Lacrosse Championship, won the NLL's 2004 Champion's Cup with the Calgary Roughnecks, won the 2005 Heritage Cup with Team Canada, NLL All-Star game Most Valuable Player in 2005, and won the Mann Cup with the Peterborough Lakers.

Kelusky certainly recognizes the huge potential a network television contract would mean to his sport. The 2005 NLL All-Star game was the perfect launch and the perfect showcase for today's pioneers.

"With a worldwide audience, this is your chance to shine. Realistically, a lot of us are playing this game for the love of it. Our sole reason for selling the sport, playing the sport, taking it to the next level. Game in and game out, when we're playing this on our mind for selling the

Tracey Kelusky
Photo by Cory Shannon

31

sport. We're trying to be the pioneers of the game and take it to the next level."

John Tavares: "(For the NLL All-Star Game in Calgary) we had a difficult travel agenda. We were on the plane for about nine hours. We pretty much went to the hotel an hour and a half before coming to the rink. We played before together. We kind of knew each other. Even if it wasn't on NBC, I'm sure it would have been the same outcome. We would have played just as hard. Thankfully it was a great game, an overtime game. Hopefully, people who had never watched lacrosse before really enjoyed it and will tune in next time. We got about an hour (sleep)."

When Jim Jennings first became commissioner, he went to all the networks.

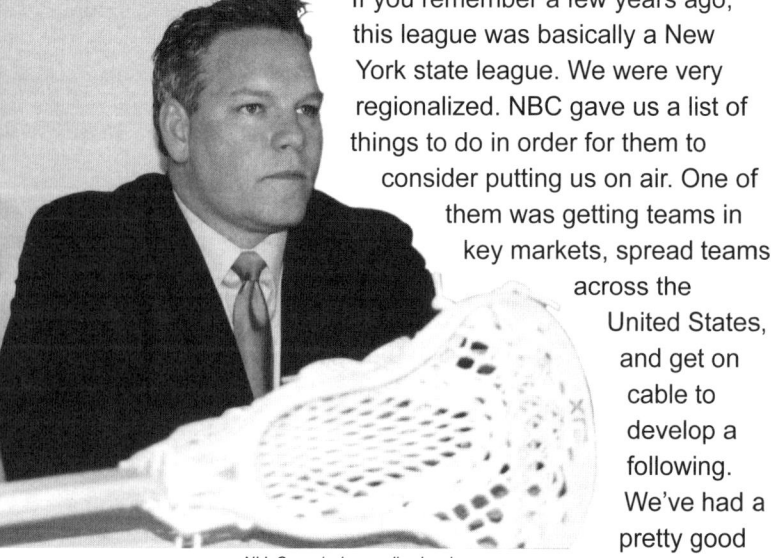

"If you remember a few years ago, this league was basically a New York state league. We were very regionalized. NBC gave us a list of things to do in order for them to consider putting us on air. One of them was getting teams in key markets, spread teams across the United States, and get on cable to develop a following. We've had a pretty good

NLL Commissioneer Jim Jennings
Photo by Debbie Elicksen

package on cable. We had to work out the other things and solidify our own issues. Once we did that, we knew we were ready for it. We engaged a company called IMG, the largest rights' buyer. Barry Frank is the co-chairman of IMG. He took the project on and really opened the doors and got us in there."

Does Jennings feel the league is in a pioneering stage right now?

"Absolutely. This (NBC deal) is a history-making event. In the U.S., network television is everything. If you're able to get yourself on network television, you get a couple things. One is credibility, which I think the league has lacked since its existence. This is finally going to give us credibility. Doors are opening where they might not have opened if we were not on network television.

"When we put a team in a market, whether it's Phoenix or Anaheim, the registration goes through the roof in that market. I think now, being on network television, registration will increase. Since we've been on TV in Canada, lacrosse associations will tell you their registrations have gone up."

The 2007 championship game aired on Sportsnet and VERSUS. The game could also be seen on pay-per-view via the NLL's Website. Casey Powell's show kicked off the radio coverage on SIRIUS.

Fox Sports Middle East will begin airing five NLL games plus the championship game during the 2008 season in Israel, Turkey, United Arab Emirates (UAE), and a number of countries in Africa. The games will be on a tape delay basis.

"The addition of NLL games on Fox Sports Middle East means our games are now seen in nearly 60 countries worldwide," reports Jennings. "We will continue to aggressively market professional indoor lacrosse to a worldwide audience."

The agreement with Fox Sports Middle East was secured by Craig Hutchison and James Swanwick of Croc Media, which handles the league's television rights in all territories beyond North America.

The 2008 season will be the first season of a two-year agreement with Eurosport to deliver an NLL game telecast to 50 countries worldwide each week throughout the regular season and playoffs.

A game's future has a direct relationship with its past. It is imperative to recognize those who made a difference and took a lead role in pioneering the game into the future. In 2006, the league opened a Hall of Fame with five charter members. They were inducted at the 2006 All Star Weekend in Toronto.

The five inaugural members were league founders Russ Cline and Chris Fritz, on-field stars Gary Gait and Paul Gait, and the winningest coach in league history Les Bartley. The 2007 inductees were players Tom "Hollywood" Marechek and Mike French; coach, manager, and former player Darris Kilgour, and writer Tom Borrelli.

The league's Board of Governors will vote on future Hall of Fame inductees, based on individual's record, ability, integrity, sportsmanship, character, and contributions of players, coaches, referees, and team and league executives, journalists, broadcasters, and others who contributed to the game of professional indoor lacrosse.

Jim Moss: "I showed back up mid-season for Albany, after not having played for five and a half years. I just had my old equipment. I had a stick with a wooden shaft. I had just returned from Australia. I had been traveling for six months. I showed up in a beat-up old pair of sneakers, wool socks, a stick that wasn't legal in the league anymore, and it was all my buddies I had played against as a kid. I show up with absolutely nothing about me that was able to play. In two weeks time, I played my first game. Six seconds into the first game, I scored a goal. I never scored another goal the rest of the season but scored one six seconds in."

Photo by Cory Shannon

PART TWO

THE GAME

"It was one of those sequestered spots outside the gates
of the world…where, from time to time, dramas of a
grandeur and unity truly Sophoclean are enacted in
the real, by virtue of the concentrated passions and
closely knit interdependence of the lives therein."
Thomas Hardy, The Woodlanders

Chapter Three:

The Game

"A man who has not passed through the inferno of
his passions has never overcome them."
Carl Gustav Jung

It's a very simple concept – put the ball in the net.
Lacrosse is easy to learn. The game is fast, involves
tempo and rhythm, and can be rough and tumble. It
combines elements of hockey, football, and basketball.

Lacrosse offers set plays, precision passing, face-offs,
man advantage, hits, and zone or man-to-man defense.
It combines football's physical hitting with hockey's
passing and basketball's shooting. Anyone can play it.

There is constant action, individual skill, physical
demands, team strategies, and conditioning.

The plays are like basketball with pick and rolls. There
are inside shots and outside shots. And the contact is
like hockey. The ball is always coming at a player's head
level and nobody wears kneepads. During a game,
players will wear upper body padding and a helmet.
Goalies are so well padded, they look three times larger
than real life.

The primary ballcarriers: passers, scorers, and feeders
are called attack men. These are your finesse players

who possess stick skills and accuracy. The midfield men or transition players are all purpose athletes who are gifted with speed and stamina. These are the team's workhorses and play both offensive and defensive ends of the field. The defensive players line up against opposition attackers. They clear the ball out of defensive zone and usually begin the transition from defense to offense after receiving an outlet pass from the goalie or by scooping a ground ball. The goalie is then the last line of defense. He also ensures that when the net is knocked off it's post, that it gets put back on so play continues. Last, there are three officials: one behind the net and two trailing the play.

"The goalie is the quarterback of the defense," describes NLL D-man Taylor Wray. Described as one of the hardest hitters in the league, Wray is a prolific collector of loose balls. Picked second overall in the 2003 Entry Draft (Calgary's first overall pick), he was named the NLL's Rookie of the Year and Co-Defender of the Year. He received a gold medal from the 2006 World Field Lacrosse championships, won the NLL's Champion's Cup in 2004, the Minto Cup in 2000 and 2002, the Founder's Cup in 1999, and just won a gold medal with Team Canada in the indoor lacrosse championships.

Photo by Cory Shannon

"Your job as a defender is to protect him and make sure that he's not seeing quality shots, that the shots he sees are from the outside, and nothing in tight. You listen to him, and he'll tell you when to step out, when to step in, when the picks are coming. The five guys in front of him act as a unit. The communication that goes on between the goaltender and the five guys up front has to be great."

Play begins with a faceoff. Two centermen place sticks back to back. The ball is placed between the two sticks and the sticks must not touch the ball. A faceoff determines possession at the start of each quarter and after a goal.

The basic premise of offense is to pass and catch, beat a defender, and shoot at the net. There are a number of offensive strategies used to find a way to beat a defender and get a shot on goal. They might include:

- Continuity offense – plays that can be reset over and over

- Set play offense – anticipating what will happen on the field beforehand

- Motion offense or the passing game – passing and cutting, using spontaneous moves

- Penetration offense or ball-control offense – one-on-one with teammates clearing a path for the ballcarrier

- Combination offense – using elements of both motion and penetration offense

Some of the moves that make the game exciting are:

- Hidden ball play: the player without the ball cradles his stick and draws the attention of the defenders and goalie, while his teammate, who actually has possession of the ball, takes the shot or passes to another teammate

- Offensive pick: is basically legal interference by an offensive player in a set position on a defender who is trying to defend against the ballcarrier

- Outlet pass: the first pass from a goaltender to start the transition from defense to offense

- Pick and roll: a player blocks or interferes, with a teammate and the defender, to free the teammate for a shot or pass; the picker then rolls out to posture for a lob pass

- Counter move: cutting to the outside of boards and eventually coming back inside to get into a good scoring position, then using the fake shot to freeze or tighten up a defender

- Strongside move: matching the defender one-on-one and then cutting to the middle

- Fast break system: five players run up the floor in an organized manner, and after getting to the right spot, look for the good shot; a five-man breakout with speed and ball control starts after the goalie makes a save, when they obtain the loose ball from playing tough defense or by intercepting a forced pass or turnover

A team can substitute a player at any point in a game if it is done on the fly. Most coaches might have a specific substitution strategy but the execution is often adjusted to what the defenders do in the game. There is a rectangular box in front of both benches called the

change area, where players must step onto when coming off the floor before they are replaced. Transition players are usually substituted the most.

Defense is simply stopping the defender and preventing a goal. Body checks are used to slow down the opponent with the ball

Photo by Cory Shannon

and must be above the waist and below the neck. A cross check (legal in lacrosse) uses the shaft of the stick to force an opponent to take a missed or bad shot.

Goalies tend to be good athletes. The position requires quick reflexes, good hand-eye coordination, the ability to pass the ball up the floor, and control loose balls. They can read a situation and fully understand concept of the game.

Teams carry a roster of 23 men but dress 18 for a game (16 runners and two goalies). Six players (one goalie and five runners) are on the floor at full strength. The game is played in four 15-minute quarters with two minutes between them plus a 12-minute halftime. Each team is allowed two 45-second timeouts per half.

A 30-second shot clock begins counting down when a team is in possession of the ball. If the team doesn't get a shot in before the clock runs out, they must turn over the ball to the other team. If they shoot and recover the rebound, they can still retain possession and the clock is reset to 30 seconds. Teams are assessed a 10-second violation when the offense fails to advance the ball to past midfield within 10 seconds of taking possession at their own end.

Box lacrosse is played in an NHL hockey rink with glass and boards intact. The playing surface is a green dieter turf carpet that is laid down over the ice surface.

In 2003, defenseman Damien Davis was the sixth African-American to be named to a first-team All-American. He was also twice named as a second-team All-American. Davis admits some turf is better than others.

"It just depends on the night. You'll get some guys rolling out turf and sometimes they'll make a mistake and they don't get it stretched out properly. There will be a gap in the corner and some on the side. It's the way that the arenas put it down. There are different styles. Some are longer. Some are shorter. Some are harder on your knees.

"Anaheim brought in a turf from New Jersey and had to black out "New Jersey" and put "Anaheim" in. When they blacked that out, they put a paint on it that is really hard. It's like a rough cement. If you fall on that, it hurts. There are sponsorship logos and seams that also alter the turf. For the most part, you don't notice anything during the game. You notice it during shootarounds. Once the game comes on, you just play."

The sticks the players use have plastic heads and aluminum or titanium handles. They are customized by each player, particularly where the ball sits in the pocket. This position determines where the ball is released (high or low). The players adjust the netting so the ball goes to the same spot each time.

The key to good stick handling is with the grasp. The bottom hand grips the stick vertically. It's held loose with the fingers with the wrist flexible enough to rotate the head. Players generally pass and catch with two hands and use the head of receiver's stick as a target.

Photo by Cory Shannon

The goal is to throw hard, crisp passes short and parallel to the floor. It's about stressing accuracy over power. The stick is never stationary. Rather the stick is cradled, moved side to side, back and forth, up and down, in a rocking motion when a player has possession of the ball. A small cradle cocks the position of the stick horizontal to the floor and is used for passing and shooting. The medium cradle is an up and down swinging motion to keep the ball in the stick. It is used for running and being in heavy traffic. The large cradle is continuous back and forth rocking with the stick held vertical to the floor. It's used to keep the ball from being jarred out when taking a cross check.

Lacrosse is at its best in the last five minutes of a game. It's when things happen. Teams down and out can somehow find their way back to score and push a game into overtime.

Kaleb Toth explains, "The last five minutes is desperation lacrosse. The team that's behind is going to the net trying to score. The team that's ahead is trying to play tough defense and control the ball. That's what makes it so exciting because it's desperation. Guys don't have another quarter to score goals. They've got to do it quick, and they've got to do it now. That's why it's a little more exciting for the fans. They're just going to the net, shooting the ball, and everything kind of happens."

John Tavares is a gifted scorer and one of the more creative players in the league with great vision. The word "legendary" is often used as a prefix to his name. He is the all-time NLL career leader for points and assists and second for the all-time goal, loose ball, and points-per-game record.

Tavares agrees that the last five minutes of a game is a special time but tough for a player.

"When it's a close game and a tough game, it's always very tiresome. I'm always tired and gasping for air. It's always very intense. There's a lot of determination from a lot of different players. You try to combine all the team's concepts and your own individual aspects. It's a big rush. It takes a lot of determination. Everyone is fighting for every little inch. You try to capitalize on every little opportunity. A lot of times when it's a big game, the crowd gets loud. You don't hear a lot of the things going on. A lot of intensity."

John Tavares: "I'm not much of a prankster myself. I'm more the responsible leader on the team and lead by example, so I try to control the pranksters on our team. But some of them do happen. One player snuck into our coaches' room and into one of the bags, took the shirt, and just drenched it in the tub. At game time, the coach would get ready for his shirt, and it was all wet. He didn't bring an extra one. Somewhere he had to scrounge up another shirt.

"Another player who doesn't play professional lacrosse – I played with him in Mississauga the year that we won. We were out in Nova Scotia where lacrosse wasn't then very popular. We were playing a lot of provincial teams and won a lot of the games handily. This player decided he was going to start searching or just looking on the floor before the face-off. He was on the floor looking for something. Of course, someone asks, 'What are you looking for?' 'My contact fell out.' There are 10 guys, two officials on the floor looking for his contact. They couldn't find it. Guys would ask him later on about his contact. He doesn't wear contacts."

Chapter Four:

Factoring Elements

"Reason is, and ought only to be the slave of
the passions, and can never pretend to any
other office than to serve and obey them."
David Hume, A Treatise upon Human Nature (1739)

League Rules

The NLL rules are reviewed annually to see how the
game might be improved to maximize fan enjoyment.

Some major rule changes are
made to open up the game to
promote more scoring.

Ball stopper Anthony Cosmo
has had one of the best save
percentage and goals against
average in the NLL. He
admits it's the goalies that
end up getting the bad end of
the stick.

Kaleb Toth (Photo by Cory Shannon)

"Being a goalie, it's not to our
advantage. It's the way you have to play. As long as our
game is moving forward then I'll take any rules."

In Kaleb Toth's opinion, most of the rule changes are to
help the American players.

"With the old rules, it was more of a Canadian style box-lacrosse game, with some field lacrosse rules in there. Now you can't pass the ball back to the goalie, the free game within three yards of the ball – those are both American field lacrosse rules. They want to make it easier for Americans to come into the National Lacrosse League and to try to sell it more to the Americans. As we all know, that's where you've got to sell sports. I don't think it's a bad thing. A couple of years ago, they had that three-yard rule in effect and the Toronto Rock absolutely killed everybody. In 1999, they won the championship. They were the only

Photo by Cory Shannon

Canadian team and would absolutely crush other teams. People were afraid to play against Toronto because, anywhere within three yards of the ball, you're allowed to hit a guy. That rule I don't think is a smart rule to bring in, because in the field game, there are no boards. If you get hit, you're just flying into open space. In the box lacrosse game, there are boards. If you get hit close to the boards, you could fly into the boards and really hurt yourself. I don't think they really thought about that too much. Time will tell. If guys start getting hurt, I'm sure they will cancel that rule."

Toth believes, however that the increase in foul times is a good call.

"You never want to hurt a guy in lacrosse. You don't want to cheap shot a guy. Accidents do happen. But that's the referee's call to decide whether it was an accident or with intent. An intent to injure, an intentional high stick, that should be a five-minute and a game misconduct. There is no time and space for that kind of play in this league. We're only allowed to dress 16 runners and two goaltenders. When a team has a five-minute major, it definitely hurts the team."

On the Floor

Players all have favorite moments: key transitions to a championship win, a great goal, playing with an idol for the first time. It's what fuels the passion for the game.

Faceoff (Photo by Cory Shannon)

You might think midfielder Pat McCready takes a back seat to fellow Buffalo Bandits stars John Tavares and Mark Steenhuis, but he is also one of the league's all stars and a Bandits go-to guy. Like most players, he's had many favorite onfield moments.

"There are so many. I guess probably one of the best things that ever happened was I was lucky enough to win a championship with "Chugger" Steve Dietrich. We played together for nine years. We beat Buffalo and had

49

a lot of my idols that I looked up to – John Tavares. Paul Gait was on our team. That was a great moment."

Kaleb Toth's moment was obviously The Goal in the 2000 final with Toronto.

"That's something a lot of kids dream about. When they're joking around on the street, it's always 3-2-1, he shoots; he scores! It doesn't matter whether it's basketball, hockey, or lacrosse. Every kid counts it down and takes that last shot. For it to happen in real life is a huge thing, and it

Photo by Cory Shannon

happened to me. It was my favorite goal in my whole career – so far.

"My favorite moment on the floor is celebrating the championship – the smiles on everyone's faces, from the fans to the owners to the training staff, the players – everyone is just so happy that all that hard work paid off and you were able to win and share something with so many people."

John Tavares' favorite moments: "It was when I played for the Mississauga Tomahawks, 1987, in our first national championship – the Founders Cup. We played against the Edmonton Miners. Played in the finals. It was a good game. I scored the winning goal for the championship. Then I would say another moment was my first Mann Cup with Brampton Excelsiors in 1992, beating New Westminster Salmonbellies. And obviously, my first National Lacrosse League championship – all my firsts. I scored the winning overtime goal in Philadelphia in 1992 with Buffalo. I think those three stand out the most."

Taylor Wray's is the 2004 championship win for the Roughnecks.

"Winning was a testament to everyone involved in the organization, from the players to the media relations, coaches, everybody. We really were a tight group. It was almost like a family. There was never a time during the season where we didn't think we were capable of competing at the highest level and winning it all. We really believed in ourselves. When it came down to crunch time, that's what got us over the edge.

"The further down the road you get, every game you win, gives you a little more confidence. Going through something as tough and as important as that brings a team together. With every win, the team gets brought closer together. Your confidence level increases. It's almost like steps on the ladder. Each step you get closer to the goal. It's kind of tough to put it into words."

Kyle Goundrey: "A teammate dove for a ball at center, and his shorts had come down. He pulled them back up, but his jock was out in front of his shorts. You could see his black shorts and a white jock.

"You see guys lose shoes and continue to play. Somebody steps on your foot and you come right out of your shoe."

PART THREE

THE BUSINESS

Like any professional sport, no matter what kind of
salary players are paid, there must be a collective
bargaining agreement. Sometimes getting both
sides to consent to the terms of that agreement
can be a challenge. It's back and forth
negotiating but the bottom line is to preserve
the league and its ability to operate and
pay players for their service.

Chapter Five:

Contracts and Agents

"You have to have a real love of your sport to carry
you through all the bad times, you still want to (play)
even when things aren't working.
Nancy Greene

Contracts

Average compensation is defined by a mutual
agreement between the league and the Professional
Lacrosse Players Association. The league-wide average
compensation for the 2004-05 season was $13,741. The
average compensation includes the aggregate sum of
the regular season salary of all roster players (exclusive
of per diems, practice pay, bonuses, and expense
reimbursement), divided by the total number of roster
players. Practice players' stipends are not included in
this calculation.

*For more detailed contract information, go to the
Professional Lacrosse Players Association Website
(www.plpa.com).*

When Brad Berrow played professional lacrosse, players
received a cut of the gate.

"Depending on how good the team did, we used to draw
pretty good. You could get a little bit of money. Of
course, you had all your gear supplied for you, traveling
expenses, and all that. The bruises, bumps, and pains

far outweighed any financial gain. We didn't care. We weren't doing it for that."

The highest paid player in the NLL doesn't make much to retire on or even live comfortably in a city like Calgary or Toronto. The money certainly continues to emphasize the fact that players play for the love of the game. Outside of lacrosse, most work other careers to make ends meet and travel on the weekend to their member teams to play.

Anthony Cosmo admits that many of the players are not used to the business side of the game.

"For us, it's really hard to negotiate our contracts. A lot of us don't have agents to do everything for us. A lot of us negotiate our own contracts. It's really tough to say how much you're really worth. If the GM says to you, we have no money; we're really short on cash; do you mind this year taking a step back? A lot of us have a good enough heart and are not really in it for the money. It's really hard to negotiate your worth with the GM because most of the GMs are your friends. It's a very close-knit family in the lacrosse world. A lot of people you know, including your bosses, are your best friends. We want this game to be personal. Although there is money involved and it is a business, we try to keep it as minimal as possible. Most of us would say if we put 18,000 in the building and not get paid, just pay for our trip out and no expenses out of our pocket, and we'd be here. We're not used to being paid and not used to being high celebrities. We're guys playing for the love of the game."

Brad MacDonald is a 2003 draft pick from the Ontario Lacrosse Association Orangeville Northmen. He says lacrosse is different from the other sports.

"You look at 95 percent of the guys in this league – they don't care what they make. They're just playing for the love of the game. It all starts when you're in minor lacrosse, then junior. You don't get paid. When you come to this league and make that extra dollar, I think it's a bonus. It's not about the money at all. We make what we make."

The league technically has a salary cap but according to Brad Banister, it's an individual salary cap.

"If you pick the maximum, which is about $23,000 U.S. and multiply by 18, that would be a cap. You don't usually hit that because there are rookies in the lineup. First-year players get a set amount; other players get everything in between. You never actually hit your cap unless you're cheating.

"Our (Roughnecks) payroll is pretty high. We have some high caliber players, but the average salary is probably around $14,000 - $15,000. The highest would be $23,000 and the lowest $6,000 plus incentives. Everything is in U.S. dollars."

Kurt Silcott says the key to the business side is to keep a strong relationship with the PLPA (Professional Lacrosse Players Association).

"We don't want to have strikes or lockouts. So far, we've been lucky enough to avoid that. The PLPA recognizes we've got to keep this game going. We've got a pretty good relationship with them. That's ongoing. We're hopeful we can eventually reach a long-term deal with them. We're going to try to learn from the other sports leagues' mistakes and also learn from the success stories they've had. The NFL is a dynamic situation. They have all their players' contracts covered by their TV. Everyone is trying to get where the NFL is.

"Our contracts are not guaranteed. It means if a player doesn't perform, he can be cut or released at any time. You don't have to pick up any remaining salary. If a player plays eight games and he's not performing, you can let him go. That player, at that point, has the opportunity to go to another team. For the players, that's a little bit of a problem, but I don't think it's that big of a problem. I think guaranteed contracts are not good. You want that player to be constantly on the edge and working hard. Most players have a competitive aspect. You don't get to this level unless you're a hard-working competitive person. The players are protected in the sense that if I were to release a guy, someone else is probably going to want him. If he's not good, then he probably doesn't deserve that money anyway."

Agents

Kaleb Toth says only about 30 percent of the players have an agent.

"I believe there are six appointed regional attorneys that can represent players and negotiate contracts for the NLL. It doesn't matter if you are an American or Canadian."

The Players' Association didn't want the lacrosse market to be flooded with agents, so it interviewed and appointed six people. According to Toth, the players with agents usually make a lot more money than the guys that don't have agents.

"The agent knows the Collective Bargaining Agreement inside and out. Usually they have other clients that are in professional sports, so they know what they're talking about, and they know what's negotiated. Our players' association pays half the cost of the fee to get an agent. I think right now the agents only charge about $350 to negotiate a contract. The players' association pays for half of that. We're trying to encourage more players to get player representatives."

Brad MacDonald experienced the process of signing with a team as weird.

"You play lacrosse for 20 years and don't really get paid for it. You never get paid for it. You step into this league: Okay, here's your contract. You think, wow. It's not a lot of money at all, but at the same time, it's pretty cool getting paid."

MacDonald didn't have an agent and still doesn't.

"If we start getting into the bigger money, that's when I'll get an agent. Right now, I think I can deal with my own. We're not talking millions here. I'm not really concerned about an agent. Our guys are good guys, and they're not trying to screw us over. I'm not really concerned."

Kaleb Toth admits the relationship between the Player's Association and management, like in any union, will have its issues. Workers always want to be paid more. Owners always want to cut costs.

"It happens in every single job. It doesn't matter if it's a car factory, teachers' association, or professional sports. Both sides have the right objective in mind: they want to grow lacrosse. Both sides are willing to sacrifice certain aspects to make that happen, to make this game more sound and strong. There are a couple things on both sides I don't agree with, but you ask any member of a union, they're never going to agree to anything 100 percent. It's one of those things where you have to look at the big picture."

The Draft

The National Lacrosse League Entry Draft consists of six rounds. The league's teams select a total of 66 players via telephone conference call. Players selected are some of the best young lacrosse talent in the United States and Canada from indoor lacrosse programs, mainly the Canadian Junior Lacrosse, which includes the Ontario Lacrosse Association (OLA) and the British Columbia Lacrosse Association (BCLA). Players are also drafted from American collegiate lacrosse programs of the National College Athletics Association (NCAA) and the National Athletic Interscholastic Association (NAIA).

The National Lacrosse League's Expansion Draft also takes place via telephone conference call. A new NLL team drafts players from the other NLL teams to begin building their inaugural season roster. Each of the member teams will submit a list of protected players to the league prior to the expansion draft. These players are considered untouchable. On that list, teams are able to protect either one goaltender and thirteen runners or two goaltenders and ten runners from its current roster.

Chapter Six:

Team Dynamics

Photo by Cory Shannon

It's one of the unavoidable elements to professional sports when teams lie on both sides of the border: travel. It also gets very expensive. Logistically for many teams, most of their players reside outside of the host city. That means a team can only practice with a full squad maybe once before a game, usually the day they bring the players in, which might be on a Friday if the team plays on Saturday. To allow for continuity and fairness across the slate, the NLL mandates that teams be only allowed to have one practice a week. For those players that do live in the team's city, they might have unofficial workout sessions, which are not technically organized practices.

"Sometimes, the price for practice can be $10,000, especially on the weekend to fly everybody in, including the coaches," admits Brad Banister. "That does not work in this league. When some players come available, you have to roll the dice and take a chance. Some of the guys flying in right now are still that valuable that we have to accommodate them."

Banister thinks Calgary, outside of Edmonton, might be perhaps the worst possible place to be playing professional lacrosse.

"Every practice we have is very costly, to bring guys in from Vancouver. And you can't ask them to quit their good jobs – some are policemen, firemen, welders, and electricians – to come out here and live. There isn't enough money in lacrosse to make a living at it."

He adds that Alberta is geographically challenged because the Roughnecks and the Rush have to fly everywhere. There are no bus trips. So when the team drafts a player, it might send out a questionnaire to ask up front if they would be willing to relocate. If they can relocate, the team might ask what their job is and if they graduated from university in order to help in the employment search. Teams want players active in the community, and there is only one way for that to happen. The player must live in the host city – but it isn't always possible.

Brad MacDonald: "When we go on the plane and you're a rookie, they call you on the PA and say, 'Can Brad MacDonald please come to the front.' They put you in a flight attendant's apron and hat. You've got to go collect garbage. I kind of did that with a smile on my face. You're kind of embarrassed. They say, 'We've got to get this guy again.' They say, 'You've got to sit in the toilet until someone has to come to use it and knocks.' That's fine. I'll do it for five minutes or whatever. So I go in there. It wasn't that busy a plane. I think I might be here for five, ten minutes. Sure enough, I get the knock. Fifty minutes later, an hour later, the flight attendant says, 'You've got to come out of there. We're going to land.' I'm in this small little bathroom for an hour. I came out of there not really smiling that much."

It's a serious issue facing teams: players that have to be flown back and forth, mostly due to the fact an NLL salary can't replace the good jobs they might already have. So the downfall is there is no attachment to the community for those particular players. The ones that do live in the city are the ones the club goes to all the time to make personal appearances.

Berrow and other scouts have been asked the question from general managers many times, 'Can that guy move here?'

"You don't want to pay a fringe player all that expense of flying him in and back out and not play him all year. There are very few teams that can afford that. You could talk a guy into moving. A lot of guys might look at the weather and say, to heck with that. I don't know if a lot of guys want to live in the United States, and that's a challenge for the American teams. There aren't enough American players to fill those teams. But it's the time zones and time off work. If you're a married family guy, and you're going to be away every weekend from middle of November until the end of April, that's tough, and you're not bringing a lot of bacon home. You're only going to be allowed to do that so long."

Anthony Cosmo teaches elementary school at home in Ontario and is one of the poster lacrosse athletes when it comes to travel. He lives in Ontario and plays for the San Jose Stealth. That means every weekend the team will fly him west to meet up with his club.

"Every game is on the road for me. I come from Mississauga. After teaching for the day, I leave straight from the classroom, go home, pick up my bags, off to a plane. It's a four-hour trip no matter where you go in the west. With the time change, it's a little bit later, so I get there about 3:00 in the morning. Then sleep and wake up bright and early and go again for another day. Then I'll go right back home. It's hectic, but it's for the love of the game. I wouldn't trade it for anything else."

Lewis Ratcliff was selected All-Pro twice and represented England in the 2007 World Indoor Lacrosse Championships. He commuted back and forth from Victoria to Calgary before he moved closer. He found a job as a personal trainer.

"For both home and away, you fly in from Victoria to the city and practice with the team that day then fly back home afterwards. You're pretty much on the road, even during home games. You're flying into Calgary, staying at a hotel. Everything is kind of messed up. Home games, you'd like to have a nice home-cooked meal before you go to the rink. It's a little awkward, but for some people, it's the only option to play in the league.

"We're still traveling together. We're still practicing and playing. We're still on the busses together. We're still out with the boys after every game. You still make good friends. You just go your separate ways afterwards. On the road, we'd normally fly back to Calgary together, and I'd hop on a plane afterwards."

Ratcliff admits there haven't been too many bad travel horror stories, just long layovers, bad connections. He's mostly had direct flights. Most of the destinations are okay for weather, such as Anaheim, Phoenix, and San Jose. But the travel schedule can definitely impact trying to find a job.

"It's tough when you're only here for four days a week. How do you go to an interview and say, 'I'd love the job, but I'm only going to work Monday to Thursday, and I might need some nights off to go to practice.' I've been really lucky. I had a great job back home just doing fundraising. My boss was awesome. Whenever I needed time off, he was good about it. I'd just make it up. For most of the guys, I think you have to have a job where you have a little bit of freedom. You can't have a set nine to five, Monday to Friday."

Pat McCready agrees you need an understanding employer.

"Flying takes a toll, too. Kyle Couling on our team (Buffalo) comes in from Victoria. Two of the days out of the week, he's traveling. I think what you're seeing here is guys who love to play the game and who are willing to sacrifice other points in their life to keep playing."

Damien Davis is a financial analyst for Brown Capital Management, Inc. in Baltimore. It's the first investment management company that is 100 percent minority owned. The airplane and hotel are his second office, where he can stay in touch via email and use the Internet for his research. He sacrifices all his vacation in order to play. He also is a volunteer coach with a middle school lacrosse team.

"When I get back (from playing), I work sometimes at night and the weekend to catch up on missed work. But it's worth it."

Kyle Goundrey is a steel fabricator at a shop that manufactures sawmill equipment in Vancouver. He's paid hourly.

"Getting time off work is an issue but somehow, everybody seems to do it. If it's switching shifts or taking holidays, I guess even calling in sick. Everybody seems to be able to get it done. You don't hear too many stories where the boss wasn't accommodating."

The bottom line is a player might not play in the NLL if he landed a career where he had to choose between his employer and lacrosse if his employer wouldn't accommodate him.

John Tavares: "Back when the league was starting, my first year was 1992 with Buffalo. I was living in Vancouver and playing summer lacrosse there. I was drafted by Detroit. At that time, you tried to accommodate most of the guys. There were only about five teams. I wasn't sure about playing in Detroit; it's about a four-hour drive from my house in Ontario, but I was living in Vancouver. Then Buffalo started a team, and they made a trade for me."

Relocation is certainly becoming a major issue, especially for newer teams. The Roughnecks didn't find a lot of players willing to move to Calgary at the beginning.

"Now that we're established, we're growing, and we're champions, maybe we can get some of these young kids who are superstars out of the junior leagues in Ontario and B.C. to come out here and start a career," adds Banister. "We're looking for guys who will relocate, put some time into the schools, perhaps get field lacrosse going, coach a minor team, and put back into the community – help kids and help coaching."

Jim Moss is one of those relocated players that coached and gave back when he played for the San Jose Stealth. He was a volunteer assistant coach with the Stanford women's lacrosse team. Moss was the NLL's defensive player of the year and a first team All-Pro in 2003, and NLL All-Star in 2004 and 2005, and earned an outdoor world championship with Team Canada in 2006. He's a player that exudes heart and character, an elder statesman to whom the rest of the league's players look up to. His day job is with STX Lacrosse, but he also has had a hand in recruiting. He describes that lacrosse involves more than just game skills.

"There are a lot of players out there that are the same player. You can find five guys with very similar styles and characteristics, in terms of how they play the game and skill level. You've established that they're a five-star athlete, but are they a five-star person? Are they a good member of the team? Are they a good person in the community? Are they responsible when it comes to drinking and partying? All those things are going to tie up a coach and a general manager's time. The less maintenance you are, the better person you are, the more that you can add in addition to just your playing ability, the better your value is."

Banister looks at what the coach wants to do with respect to transition, offense, or defense and builds a team around that format.

"When we started four years ago, we wanted to win the championship right away. That put a lot of pressure on all of us to do that. Sometimes, you make some trades that the coaching staff doesn't agree with, but it turned out for the best. We gave up our first rounders to get what we needed. The first year wasn't very competitive; the second year got a little better; the third year, we

made the playoffs. For me, it was a gamble. I wanted to win right away, so I wasn't building a team over five or six years. We gave up a lot of stuff to get a lot of guys. Since then, we've got those draft

Photo by Cory Shannon

picks back anyway. That's the way to do it: stick your neck out a little bit, give up some things and trade down the road."

Scouts look for players with a lot of guts, who can deal with pain and aggression – but not to the point where they're doing something stupid. They have to have an intense desire to win and a very hard work ethic.

"The best lacrosse players I've ever played with are there before practice and there after everyone leaves, working on the basics of the game," says Berrow. "You can do the fancy stuff well, but it's being able to do the basics. It doesn't matter how much talent you have, there is no substitute for work. If you're not physically fit, you're not mentally sharp."

The last five minutes of the third period is very telling as to how fit a player is. The team counts on a player to go hard when the game is on the line. It counts on its skill players to get things done when it's tight and tough. The players that come through do so because of hard work.

"You can't make that perfect shot unless you've had lots of practice. You have to be prepared to give, sacrifice. I've seen guys going up for loose balls, jumping up in the air, and extending themselves; they get cut in two when they're extended. Crawling off the floor and going back out again – that's what it takes to win a championship."

> *Pat McCready: "I wasn't drafted. I was a very defensive-minded player in junior. I got a walk-on tryout with the Buffalo Bandits. I was the last cut. There was an opportunity that opened up in Charlotte, North Carolina for an expansion team down there. I packed everything up and moved down and made a go of it. I think at the time, we were getting paid about $200 a game. Just to try and live off that. There were some unique challenges. Lucky enough, they folded and I moved back to Rochester and got traded back to Buffalo." (Did the team pay for his trip to North Carolina?) "It was kind of like, get down there and we'll see. Then they took care of you a little bit when you got down."*

For new players being brought into the league, the difference between college and professional lacrosse involves many things. The athletes are older and more physically mature. They're better, bigger, faster, and stronger. Coaching is better. The system is more intense, and you start playing in front of larger crowds.

Kaleb Toth admits the transition from junior to professional lacrosse was difficult.

"You go from playing with boys to men. You're 18, 19, or 20 in junior and playing with other 18 to 20 year olds. When you go to pro, you're playing with guys from 20 to 40 years of age. They have more experience. They know what they're doing."

Brad MacDonald came in from college and found it tough.

"You go against a guy like Tracey Kelusky compared to a good goal scorer in high school or in junior, there is a 100 times difference. You've got to adapt. You've got to change your game style. It's a lot of work. When you make that jump to professional, no matter what the sport, you're playing against better players, bigger guys."

Luke Gilbert: "The Entry Draft was a little rough for me just because I didn't play up north in Canada. I only played in college. I played two years in Division I, was two-time All-American. I played in plenty of summer leagues. As far as the Draft, no one really knew me or if I was going to be able to play in the indoor leagues because I'm lanky. I went in the fifth or sixth round with the Stealth. They told me they were going to draft me, but I didn't know when. Since there weren't other teams really looking for me, they felt that no one *knew who I was – that they were safe. You only get drafted once.*

"It's a lot easier when you come into anything as a sleeper, when people aren't ready for you versus someone first round. Like Ryan Boyle, when he goes out on the field, they will be most physical with him because he is a top prospect, and they want to rough him up. He's American. He's not ready for the game – they think."

Brad MacDonald: "I was drafted 23rd overall. I was in a prep school in the U.S. and looking to go to college. It was a little too expensive, so I kind of looked at this as an option. I thought I'd give it a try. I didn't pressure myself to make it. I just kind of came into camp with a relaxed attitude.

"My dad coaches in this league – with Philadelphia. When he was with Ottawa, he says, 'Why don't you get into the draft?' I said, 'Yea, I'll put my name in.' Two months later, I got the call in the morning from Dave Bremner and Chris Hall. They said, 'Congratulations, you've been drafted.'

"I kind of overlooked it. Some people get drafted, and they don't really do much. It was more of a pride thing – getting drafted as a professional. When I thought about it, I thought I'd give it a shot."

PART FOUR

THE PLAYERS

"Man is only truly great when he acts from the passions."
Benjamin Disraeli

Ideally, speed, quickness, agility, size, and strength are what make a great player great. He also encompasses those intangible qualities, like leadership, character, sportsmanship, and integrity. He'll have a combination of athletic and lacrosse ability – having the conditioning and stamina to finish a game and excellent lacrosse sense in being able to make split-second on-field decisions.

In looking at the various positions, the talent breakdown for each would be:

Goalie: courageous, no fear of being hit, quick reaction, a team leader, engineer – directs the position of each man on defense, and able to organize and execute clearing everyone to the offensive half of the field

Photo by Cory Shannon

Defense: a team defender, strong athleticism, has size, strong, has great footwork, has an element of toughness, ability to cover the ball, understanding of defensive strategies, great anticipation, unselfish, and lots of patience

Midfield: is athletic, has stamina and endurance, understands team defense, reacts quickly, agile, understands offense, and has scoring skills

Attack: the primary scorer, great stick work, is athletic, has a great understanding of offense, can finish, takes punishment well, agile, has maneuverability and speed

Lacrosse systems have no bearing on whether a player is good or not. It's about being strong in the basic skills of the game, which they have developed through practicing the little things. They are a student of the game.

Qualities of a one-on-one player include quickness, balance, power, intelligence, deception, and the ability to beat people naturally without thinking.

Forward Lewis Ratcliff looks at the great players in the league to compare.

"It's the ability to perform every night. You look at someone like Gary Gait or John Tavares, they've been three goals and three assists every game for the last 10 years. That's what I want to be as a player – a more consistent player. You don't necessarily have to have the six-, seven-goal games, but you have to come and play every night. When I think of a great player like a Tracey Kelusky or a John Grant, they're there every night. They never take a night off."

Confidence builds consistency. Ratcliff explains, "If I go to the rink and say, 'I hope I score a goal tonight,' then the confidence isn't there. If I go to the rink and say, 'I'm going to score, you can't stop me,' that's the mindset those guys have."

Confidence is a huge factor in playoff lacrosse, having that winning swagger, the confidence coming into the room. You know you are going to win.

Kaleb Toth knows a positive attitude also has a lot to do with it, as does hard work.

"A lot of those skilled players that keep playing work hard. They work hard from when they're 21 to 40. It's because they train. They're in great shape, focused. They're very smart players. They go over the videotapes. They know the advantages. They know other teams and players' weaknesses. That's why you see a lot of these veteran players stick around for a long time. They know their opponent.

"While every player may not be that diligent, a lot of them are. Going over game tape, you watch for a goalie's weaknesses, what their defense tends to do, their power play. You break down and analyze each aspect and learn what every team is good at and what their weak points are. Then you try to exploit them during the game. The key is being prepared. Lacrosse is a game that switches momentum. In one minute, you can be up three goals, a moment later, you can be down three."

> Kaleb Toth: "When they announce your name and you run out with the spotlight on you, it's a big rush of adrenalin. You get goose bumps. The whole crowd starts cheering. It's a real special feeling. During the game, you don't really notice them. At least I don't. I tend to block everything out. One of the greatest examples I give to people, if you've ever seen that movie 'For the Love of the Game,' Kevin Costner is a pitcher. Right before the first pitch, the crowd is going nuts and everything. He looks at the catcher, zooms in on his glove, and everything else shuts right down. He doesn't hear the crowd. All he sees is that catcher's mitt. That's kind of exactly how it is. Everything seems to go quiet. You are so focused on the game."

Jamey Bowen has been a longstanding lacrosse icon in Edmonton, heavily involved in the game's youth development. He scored the Rush's very first goal in the history of the franchise – at 8:50 of the first quarter in a 10-9 overtime loss against San Jose on January 6, 2006. Not only is he a teacher, Bowen is also a restaurant and bar owner of three Edmonton establishments. He talks about his approach to the game.

"The pro game you break down and you've got so much detail. It's a great game. It's poetry. The goals in this game are better than any other goals I've seen. In basketball, there are so many baskets. Unless you see one big dunk, that's pretty much it. In lacrosse, if there are 20 goals, 16 are beautiful. Lacrosse is all finesse."

Jim Moss admits when he played professional ice hockey, before he played professional lacrosse, he wasn't very skilled.

"But I worked so much harder than everybody else. I was so consistent that I had a coach tell me one time, even if I couldn't skate, he would use me as an example to the rest of the players as to what you should be doing."

Talent did open the lacrosse door for Moss, but it wasn't the key ingredient to making a team. You had to be consistent. You had to have character.

"You can't take a night off because that might be the very night the person is there who can make or break you."

Experience, a love for the game, the passion to get better – all these things also play into what makes a strong player. The personality of a player can make or break a team. Organizations want to avoid the "poison in the locker room," that player that continuously complains and puts a rift in the room. Or the player that is continually in trouble with the law, substance abuse, and has a lack of work ethic, even if he's a star.

Inside the dressing room, a team is built from the personality of its players. Brad Berrow knows a team has to be careful about the type of players it's selecting.

"It's not necessarily the most skilled players; it's the people with the strongest characters. On any winning team that I've been on, some of the best team players we've had were somewhat of the less skilled. They're the ones that give the most. We had our leaders in terms of ability. But the people we looked up to the most were the ones that drove themselves the most in games."

To field a real winning team, players accept putting the team first. That means if his style of play isn't suited to a particular opponent, that player would be willing to sit on the bench. Or a player will go into a corner, knowing he'll probably get hurt. He will do all the other activities outside of the rink, such as the extra practice.

Brad Berrow: "In the old days, we had the leather sticks. The players are bigger and faster, now. There's less hitting. Now the sticks are plastic and metal. Some of the smacks sound great but they don't hurt as much. In using the old wood sticks with not so good a padding, the strikes would hurt more. Now, it's place and push. As you master the league, there's more hitting allowed. In the old days, it was a slash, followed by a crosscheck. If you hit yourself with a hollow metal object, it's not going to hurt as much as if you deliver that same blow with a wood object. In the old days, before they brought in helmets, there was no checking above the shoulders. Today, the hitting is less. The guys are faster. The padding is better."

In John Grant Sr.'s professional playing days, you would never see players from opposing teams drinking in the same bar. However, today, players get to know each other very well. They might be on the same summer lacrosse team. Grant Sr. sees them as being very down to earth.

"They go to work the next day. They're amongst the people. They're not afraid to answer questions or sign autographs. They don't jump into their SUV and scream out of the parking lot. It's not a million dollar sport. These guys play in the summer for basically the love of the sport, and for the thrill and the experience to play in front of 17,000 people. Then they get up and go to work. Some are cops; some are teachers. They have the respectability in the community. It's a 16-game schedule. They're giving up their weekends. The show that they're putting on is unbelievable. Where can you go to get that entertainment for $15?"

Tracey Kelusky's best friend is John Grant Jr. Kaleb Toth has friends on other teams in the east division and west division.

"The thing about lacrosse players is we leave it on the floor. After the games, we have our post-game parties, and everyone has a beer together. Everything is kept on the floor. After the game, everyone just tries to sell the sport. It's entertaining for the fans."

The NLL has a mandate that is unlike any other sport. The players have endorsed it and believe it is a key to selling their game. Regardless of the outcome, after every NLL game, both the home and visiting teams send players back out onto the floor to sign autographs for the fans. Then once the media interviews are done, the players are back in from the floor autograph sessions, they head up to the arena pub where they socialize with more fans and each other over a beer.

Photo by Cory Shannon

"We preach so much how our guys are accessible, how our guys are just regular people, and we work jobs like Mom and Dad work jobs," says Moss. "We use the comparison that we're like super heroes. The guys are like Clark Kent Monday to Friday. They go into the phone booth and come out as Superman on Friday night and Saturday night. They do things that Mom and Dad can't do and still maintain the humble nature that Mom and Dad have because they work for everything that they have. If we're going to preach that now, the thing that we can't afford to do is become hypocrites as soon as we get a little taste of fame, a little bit of growth and success in our league, that it all becomes diluted. As lacrosse players, coaches, and league officials, it's part of our culture. We need to make a commitment that when we do grow, we're going to remember all the things that made us grow and stay with them."

That said, certainly one might appreciate that players might not be as enthusiastic about signing autographs after a loss. But Moss says it's no excuse. He remembers when the Stealth only won four games one season.

"But do you know what? When you've only won four games, you haven't been giving your fans what they deserve. So guess what? You better stay twice as long and sign autographs. If they're still willing to ask for your autograph and wait around to talk to you after the game, when you've just lost and they paid good money to see you, you had better be there to sign the autographs. It's tough. The coach comes in and rips a strip off you. You're beat up. But the same goes in life, when you're beat up the most is when you've got to suck it up and put on a happy face. You keep going."

John Grant Sr.: "I was coaching a pee wee team and took 11 kids down to Philadelphia in a van. At that time, the manager of the Spectrum – they don't have real bacon in the States – I told him I'd bring him a pound of bacon if he'd let us in. We went down, and on Friday night, we got to see the Chicago Bulls and Michael Jordan. Then on Saturday, the Flyers were playing New Jersey. We had tickets. Then I had to play in the league on the Saturday night. The kids stayed at the hotel near the Spectrum. On Sunday, we went over and one of the people, who used to be with the Wings, let them in Vet Stadium. They were running around and were given souvenirs. They were at center ice, were given hockey sticks, pucks. It was a three-day weekend that was unbelievable. The kids, to this day, talk about that experience."

Chapter Seven:

Commitment

"Sports do not build character. They reveal it."
James Michener: Sports in America (1976)

While many players do keep some of their jobs to, in essence, "fund" their love of playing lacrosse, even with the clubs paying for commuting to and from games and other perks, there are many sacrifices one makes.

Players are always on the move. A lot of times it's difficult to find connections to a city, especially to get a career going if you don't already have one.

Kaleb Toth doesn't think he's sacrificed too much. He hasn't given up anything for the game. The biggest thing is missing his family while being away every weekend.

"Sure, I haven't been able to go out as much as those I grew up with, who have traveled the world, but I look at all the stuff that lacrosse has given to me. I don't look at what it's taken away from me. I think every athlete's like that. There will always be a time in your life when you can travel and do different things. Everyone comes in the moment right now. Lacrosse is my moment. I'm going to do it until the moment is gone and then work on the next moment.

"A lot of guys have gone to university on lacrosse scholarships. Because we don't get paid full-time money to do the thing that we love, everybody has to work. We have guys that are firefighters, police officers, teachers – everyone does everything. They work and try to make ends meet. Lacrosse is more of a part-time job. One day, hopefully, you'll get to see guys play in a 40-game schedule, getting a couple hundred thousand – enough to live off. But I don't see that happening for at least another 10 years or so."

Jim Moss speaks to kids about the commitment it takes to become an athlete.

"They just assume you can pick something up and make it yours. It's certainly not that easy. A lot say how lucky we are to be professional lacrosse players and say the same about every professional athlete. You're so lucky to do what you do. And we are lucky, but there are so many sacrifices along the way.

"When other kids have quit their sport and they're out drinking and partying, we're still doing our sport. We give up our weekends in the summertime to play our sport and get better at it. We're in the gym for two hours after school. They're out fooling around or going to the bar when you're in that development stage. That's really what makes the difference. What kids are willing to do more of when it really counts – at the development stage in high school and college."

Casey Powell: "In my rookie year, we went up to play the Toronto Rock at Maple Leaf Gardens. It was sold out. I remember at halftime walking into the locker room and our captain was in the showers smoking a cigarette. It just goes to show you they are every day guys. I thought it was pretty shocking at first but pretty funny."

The Money

Jamey Bowen says playing professional lacrosse means giving up the big paycheck you could be earning elsewhere.

"It's pro in every aspect other than the money. You're supposed to be this pro athlete. Everybody has the extra job. I've taught for 10 years. When we scored our first goal, I had all these press clippings. Monday, I got in my minivan and went back to school. It was just back to reality. You're never going to get the highest of conditioned athletes. We just can't do that until the money is there and guys don't have to worry about anything else. You miss work to come play lacrosse. You're taking a pay drop. Until that really changes or something is done with that, it just won't be the baseball, hockey, or football.

"The money is not going to change anything. I'm older, so it's not really going to affect my life. I have to definitely weigh out the odds of the time away from the kids and my wife versus playing. She has been good to let me play. I'd like to play more, but it is a big commitment. We go five days a week. It would just be nicer if they could really take it to the next step with more teams, really get it into more TV markets, pay the guys $100,000 so they could live and really commit to this. The level is here, and I think you can just see it soar. It needs more owners like Bruce Urban – guys who can take a chance, who have big bucks, who aren't on a shoestring budget. No one can take over an NHL team with a shoestring budget. You'd lose your $100 million. A couple of the teams in the league are a little light in the pockets. No offense to them. They took the chance. You need more big time bucks. You look at Colorado. It's through the roof. He can afford it if only 10,000 come, but he's got it marketed everywhere. Toronto, I think, sells itself. You can't have pro and be minor league owners."

Playing With Pain

Anyone who has watched an NLL game might imagine how many bumps and bruises a player will ice afterwards. In rough and tumble action, scrambles around the net, and players running full board, injuries happen. Some are more serious than others but likely most play through the pain. It's something to think about when it appears as if a player is having a bad game. Perhaps he's only operating at 60 percent.

Brad Banister doesn't think the injuries are all that bad.

"On the dangerous side of sport, I think we fall behind ping pong. We lose a lot of knees at the professional level because the carpet is so sticky and these guys are going so hard. On the concrete and outdoors, there's a little more slip to it. You hardly see any injuries."

Of course, the issue is if you do hurt yourself in a game, you still have to go to work on the job the next day.

Brad Berrow has witnessed his fair share of injuries.

"I've seen guys destroy shoulder muscles, having to pick their hand up to put their stick into it, and they'd only run one way and just go kill penalties. They're living through that pain because they want to win and are probably never able to do it again. You don't have a great deal of time to play this sport."

Being in good shape helps players recover from injuries. Being out of shape can lead you to being out of position, which is when you could get hurt more often. But then part of playing professional lacrosse means you also have to be willing to get hurt. It's going to happen. When you play on Friday or Saturday night, chances are you'll be feeling it on Sunday.

Box lacrosse has more injuries (than field) that come from the restraints of the boards. There's nowhere to hide.

Jim Moss has seen his fair share of medical problems.

"You're talking to the right guy when you talk about wear and tear. I've got really terrible feet. The turf has just been eating them up. I have collapsed arches, bunions, and you name it. It's kind of a league joke about how bad my feet are. There's a direct example of wear and tear on a lacrosse player."

John Tavares is grateful he hasn't been seriously injured.

"One year, I tore my MCL (medial collateral ligament in the knee), which forced me to miss one game. Of course, you get your bumps and bruises, sprained ankles, bad hips, whatever it might be. Once the game gets going, your adrenaline gets going and you kind of forget about it. There are some injuries that slow you down. I definitely feel my injuries don't heal as fast anymore. The adrenaline doesn't kick in as quickly as it used to. You're out there and just want to do your best.

Now, I know if I'm injured, I've got to be careful and not make any stupid mistakes to try and push it. Whereas before, I'd be a little more reckless and play through it. I think most of the guys in lacrosse are like that."

Damien Davis says turf issues cause a lot of injuries.

"Turf toe, stingers, broken fingers, and broken wrists are rare but more common than not. The more serious is you can get your knee blown out. With box, they're rolling the turf up and rolling it out. There are some wrinkles out there you can get caught on which are dangerous. A lot of people have problems with turf burn, especially because the turf is dirty. People are sweating, bleeding, and spitting. When you do get a burn, it's not a very "clean" environment. You have to take care of turf burn right away."

Kaleb Toth admits the body gets worn down from traveling and playing. Back to back games take a toll. The body takes a beating and needs a week to recuperate. There also isn't any protection on the legs.

"When you fall on the turf, it's like falling on sandpaper. A lot of guys put Vaseline on their knees. When they hit the turf, they kind of slide, and the Vaseline gives them a little protective coating so they don't tear off the skin."

Kyle Neufeld was drafted by Arizona in 2003 and won two Minto Cups in 2001 and 2003. He tore his ACL (anterior cruciate ligament), the main ligament that gives the knee its stability, in his first year. One of the most serious of athletic injuries, an ACL injury takes up to a full year to rehabilitate.

"When I was in training camp with Arizona, I ran a V-pick, so I ran one way and cut the other way. That's when it just folded. I heard a pop and continued to play. I could feel there was something wrong. It wasn't preventing me from running. Just as time went on, I knew there was something wrong with my leg."

Neufeld saw two different surgeons, who initially diagnosed it was his quadracept and figured his hamstring would be able to support his knee. That wasn't the case. He took three months off from training camp, but when he went back to his first practice – pop. This time, it didn't swell as much, but as soon as he heard it, he lost all strength in his knee.

"It got really wonky and Jell-O-y. Eventually, I told the surgeon, I need to get this done. They went into my knee, and I had a completely torn ACL."

The ligament was replaced. But because it took so long to get diagnosed and he waited so long to get the surgery done, there was some damage.

He continued to go to therapy to strengthen it, which was the advice from his doctors.

"When I initially hurt my knee, I was living with my parents, so making my own meals and leaving for work to pay the bills wasn't an issue. I could take time off work. When I had surgery done, I was living on my own. At the time, I had a wonderful girlfriend who was able to take care of me. If I didn't have anyone to help me out, I don't know what I would have done. After surgery for a couple of weeks, I was bedridden. If it wasn't for my girlfriend, I wouldn't have been able to heal.

"It can be tough sometimes. You're up on your feet, and you just want to lie down. It's a lot of trouble getting around for the first couple of weeks. If you're able to get on the crutches and get comfortable right away, you're fine.

"When I initially hurt my knee, I worked in a warehouse. I would drive a truck during the day. Then I couldn't drive, as it was my right leg. I couldn't really lift anything. There was other work I did that didn't require heavy lifting. I was able to put in a few hours, and really that's all it was to get out of the house. Once I had my surgery done, I worked in an office. I could just work on my computer."

After missing that first season with Arizona, Neufeld was traded to Calgary after the surgery, which caused him to miss his second season.

"It was definitely frustrating. Just watching the game can be frustrating because you want to get out there. You're still training and working with the stick, but you're not playing."

He won a Minto Cup in 1986, the Mann Cup in 1989, 1991, and 2001, and was the Mann Cup MVP in 2001, but Andy Ogilvie is really a medical miracle. He has had five, count them, five knee surgeries. He had his ACL redone on his left knee in Buffalo, back in 1999.

"Everything was fine, as long as you keep your muscles strong. Everything was going well for me. The way it happened was I was on a face-off. The ball sort of came out in the middle. I was running towards the middle, running beside my guy, a couple of guys coming towards me. A player sort of fell down and rolled into my knee.

The turf is 100 percent traction, so my foot didn't move. My knee bent backwards. It popped. It actually sort of went in and out. You could actually feel it go in and out of joint. It's the most pain I've ever had in my life."

Ogilvie attests that timing of getting looked after depends on who you know. Fortunately for him, his own personal doctor was the president of the Coquitlim Adanacs of the summer league.

"I was on crutches for a few weeks. The accident happened on February 4. Because of his connections, I had the operation on February 22. That's pretty quick.

Andy Ogilvie (Photo by Cory Shannon)

"It was a bad rehab because it was the second time around. The original time I had it done in the States – a patella tendon (the ligament doctors used to replace the ACL). It was screwed into my bone at both ends. I actually had to phone Buffalo and find out what kind of screwdrivers that they could use to take the screws out. They did the hamstring tendon this time."

This second surgery was not a simple operation. His knee had a lot of fluid. The rehab took a long time.

"I've had five knee operations, two on the left and three on the right. When you're on crutches, you can't do anything. You can't carry anything. I spent the first two weeks on painkillers and probably slept for 16 hours a day, icing my leg, not just when I was awake. I went to sleep with an icepack on my leg.

When both Ogilvie's knees were bad:

"I came back to Canada. They send you to physiotherapy right away. My muscles were quite strong. I could walk, but they wanted me to use crutches. I could sort of hobble. My physiotherapist at that time told me to only get one knee operated on at a time. He didn't know how I was going to do the rehab. But I offered to do both knees at the same time – two rebuilt knees at the same time. That was unprecedented, I guess. I didn't want to go through a whole year (of rehab). I'd rather go through just six months. Yea, that was bad. They gave me two ice coolers with hoses that went up to the pads I put on my knees. I had to sleep with both knees elevated and a cooler on each knee. I had to do that for about six weeks. That was a tough one."

Ogilvie has had more than knee injuries during the course of his career. In 2001, when he played for Buffalo, his 240-pound buddy from Vancouver cross-bodied into his knee. While he thought his leg was broken, it turned out to be just cartilage damage. He had his collarbone permanently separated in 2004, and in 2003, he broke his hand in a fight.

"Being fit as an athlete can help with the rehab process. I think that makes a big difference. The stronger your muscle is, the easier it is on your joints. I work out at least three four days a week, sometimes five at the gym. It's sort of my attitude that I will work to make my muscles strong. That's going to actually take the pressure off the joints of the knee. Athletes probably have an advantage in that they know what to do and when to do it.

"Physiotherapy is not a fun thing. They're goofy little exercises but they do work. You have to believe in the exercises and have to be willing to do them. A person who is not athletic and doesn't like to work out, it would be a longer, slower process.

"A blown ACL is going to take a certain amount of time no matter how hard you work. You can't start off the bat doing squats, lunges, or anything like that. You start out small. You can't really rush recovery. Your knee just won't take it. You have to start out with the little small exercises. If you do the big exercises, you're going to actually do more damage. One of the biggest problems I had was I had a lot of fluid on my knee from the operation. The fluid prevented me from bending my knee for a while. I had to do the little exercises first. If I started doing the big exercises, that would put more fluid on my knee. There's no quick route back."

Devan Wray won two ACC championships with Duke University, was with the Canadian Junior field lacrosse team in 1996 and 1999, won a Minto Cup in 1998 and 2000, and won the Champions Cup in 2004.

"You get whacked during the game, so a Charlie horse that's real bad, you don't even notice it. You have bumps and bruises going into the game but as soon as you get through warm-up, and the opening whistle blows, maybe it's just me personally, but I don't even think about that sort of stuff. It just goes away. Then you sit down at half time or at the end of the game, once your focus goes away from lacrosse and competition, when you're relaxing after the game, that's when the bumps, bruises, and pain start to resurface. I don't even notice until the end of the game when you're taking your gear off and you have a sore shoulder, a big bruise on your arm."

Wray missed the 2005 season rehabbing through ACL surgery. He admits there is that element of hesitation when you step onto the field after such a devastating injury. It's not always easy to feel confidence in your ability, even though you've received the go-ahead from the doctors and trainers.

"I think when you first step on the field, that's the toughest part to get over. You can do as much training in the gym, lifting, biometrics, and stuff like that. Until you step on the floor and start running around with your team again, you don't know how your knee's going to react or your shoulder, your wrist. It's definitely a confidence thing. It's a mental thing. That's the toughest part. Coming back from any injury and forgetting that it was hurt. Your knee is strong. Your elbow is strong. Just go out and play. With repetition, that inkling gets weaker and weaker and weaker until it's gone. That's the position you want to be in, when you're trying to go full throttle.

"Conditioning is a huge factor. It's real easy, especially after a major operation, like a knee operation, to sit on your butt and get fat or something. As soon as the brace is off, it's on the bike, even if it's something light, just to keep my knee moving. For a certain period of time, there's nothing you can do. As soon as that brace is off, staying in good shape and keeping your conditioning up is paramount to having success with trying to get back to the position where you can step on the floor again."

Taylor Wray: "I've seen that happen in games where somebody slips and falls and their shorts slip around their ankles. You fall down a lot more in lacrosse than some other turf games. When you fall or slide in lacrosse, your shorts have a tendency to come down."

Longevity

"What I know most surely about mortality and
the duty of man I owe to sport."
Albert Camus

To be an elite player, one needs strength, endurance, agility, flexibility, and quickness. Making it past scores of other athletes to become an NLL player doesn't mean squat. It's only the beginning. You can be in the buffest of shape at age 20, but as you turn 26 and older, there are likely more players waiting in the wings to take your spot.

Brad MacDonald agrees you can never relax.

"Once you're here, you can't really relax because there is always someone who can take your job. We have four or five guys that aren't in the lineup every night, so if you don't play that well in one game, you can have your spot taken."

Jim Moss adds that once you've made it, you can't rest on your laurels; you have to work doubly hard to stay in the game.

"That's not even to advance further into the ranks to the All Star level. I had not picked up a stick in five and a half years. I had been playing hockey that whole time. They knew I could play the game. I definitely maintained the skill level to get into the lineup, but how good was I going to be? I made the commitment that I would throw 1,000 balls a week against the wall, left hand and right hand. I came back, and it's kind of a joke that I'm always using my weak hand – practicing with it. A few years ago in the All Star game, I'm cutting through the middle on my offside, the ball comes to my weak hand, I grab it, and I can throw an around-the-world shot with my weak hand and score a goal. That's an example of something that wouldn't have existed if it weren't for working hard. I tell every kid that asks me how they can get to the NLL: work hard and do more than everybody else. The same holds true for myself. If I want to be better than the rest of the guys in the NLL, I've got to work harder and work longer."

But how do guys like John Tavares and Gary Gait do it? How do they stay in the game as long as they have and stay competitive? Of course, being a student of lacrosse helps. Practice helps. Perseverance helps. But there is really only one thing that will keep an athlete in the game for even one season, not just 10 or 20 and that's conditioning.

"Once you get older, everyone knows it takes a lot more work to stay in shape," admits Kaleb Toth. "Definitely, when you're an older athlete, you've got to keep working out. Sometimes, you don't need to be the fastest guy out there. You can see a play happening before it actually happens. You get yourself set up in the right position. When you get these young guys coming up, they seem to be full of piss and vinegar, run all over the place and they never seem to lose wind. When you're older, you learn to conserve your energy. You learn to be a little wiser when you do go. You don't just go all the time. Maturity is a big thing in any sport."

The older players get, the more they have to train. We're not just talking about lifting weights here. It's an overall fitness regime that helps athletes minimize weariness, plan for success, prevent injuries, and help them stay mentally tough enough to endure the physical aspects of the game.

Part of conditioning includes little things like stretching, although it's not something many of us are crazy about. But trainers will tell you that stretching does help prevent injury by reducing strains, spasms, and muscle tears.

A warm-up might include a light jog, jumping rope, stationary bike, running backward, and sideway running. All of these elements play a huge role in longevity.

Tracey Kelusky will attest, "The job of a lacrosse player is to practice and play, conditioning the rest of the time. If you keep up to maintain the conditioning, you have more of a chance to keeping a spot on the team."

For a guy like Jamie Bowen, who is married with two kids and three bars, he knows keeping up physically is something he has to do regardless of his busy schedule.

"I'm 36. Most of these guys are 23. For me to be even close to competing, I've got to stay in shape. I've never been the guy that took conditioning seriously or stretching. Now because of my age, I've really got to."

Kurt Silcott: "When my brother first started playing for Buffalo, at that time, I didn't know about this Canadian game. I went to a Bandits game at the Buffalo Auditorium. I didn't know what to expect. My brother was telling me it was going to be sold out. I was thinking that all the field lacrosse games I had been to, there were maybe 1,000 people watching. He's telling me there's going to be 16,000 people packed in the Aud. So I call a bunch of buddies. We buy a bunch of tickets. It was absolutely crazy. People were screaming and yelling – a packed house. I thought, wow. This is really amazing. The game was over, and my brother had told me about some of the guys on the team. 'John Tavares, he's the best player in the world. Gary Gait…this and that…the top guys.' I told him I'd meet him outside the locker room. I come down outside the locker room, and in the Aud, on the floor level, there's all these pathways and turns. I didn't really know where I was going. I told my buddies I'd meet them at the bar, but I'll find my way down to my brother. I'm walking along the floor in the back of the house. I don't know where I'm going. I see this guy and turn to him. He's got equipment on. I say, 'Hey, buddy. Can you tell me where the Bandits' locker room is? I need to find my brother.' He says, 'Oh, you've got to be Brian's brother.' We looked pretty similar. 'It's back over this way.' And he shows me. I'm walking back over with this guy and don't know who it is. It turns out it was John Tavares. Ten years later, I'm his GM."

Chapter Eight:

Canada Versus U.S.

Luke Gilbert admits there's a "we/they" thing between Canadians and Americans inside the locker room.

"Oh, yea. Definitely. It's kind of funny. A couple years ago, I think we only had four Americans on the team. I was definitely the outcast the first year in the league. The group we had was a tight-knit group. They were used to dealing with each other and knew how each other worked. They weren't that open to newcomers. The next year, we pretty much have four or five guys left from the team before. Everyone came in the same boat. We meshed. We gelled. There were really no egos on the team, but at the same time, there's the whole Canada-U.S.

"It's kind of cliquey. All the U.S. guys will tell stories. Canadians will use different lingo. We have no idea. They call this place (arena) a barn – things like that to throw you off. It's funny to work together.

"I was definitely one of the outcasts. I was on the outside. I was on the practice squad. I didn't really get any respect. I practiced a lot and picked up my game. I went from being a two-time All-American to nothing. Luckily, we got a whole new batch of guys for a clean slate. I was really able to be myself with everyone."

John Grant Sr. says for a lot of Americans, lacrosse is like soccer.

"The soccer people like the field soccer, and the traditionalists don't like indoor soccer. That's the same situation for lacrosse. The box people really don't like field lacrosse, and the field people don't like box lacrosse."

Regarding the lacrosse opportunities in U.S., Damien Davis says it was all outdoor lacrosse from recreational league, middle school, high school, and then college.

"I didn't play box until I graduated."

The differences between the two games is everything.

Davis comments, "Six on six, instead of ten on ten. In field, you play on a soccer field; in box, you play in a hockey rink. There's a little bit more contact in box, higher scoring. For field, you can be more of a two-hand player. In box, you can get away with being one-hand dominant and stay on one side of the floor. Other than that, it's basic lacrosse – shoot for the corners, still have that dodge-hard quickness athletic ability. All these things carry over to box and visa versa.

"There's a little trash talk back and forth. For the most part, they're calling us war-mongers. They're the neutral guys. It's all in good fun."

In comparing box versus field, Kurt Silcott looks at it as really the same game.

"I think there's a little misconception by players. Part of it is a bit of an ego thing. The Canadians feel their game is better, and that's the true game in the way to play lacrosse. The Americans feel the same way about their game. It's natural. Their skills, over time, have developed their particular game. This is a broad statement, but the Canadians are probably better with sticks in close quarters, and the Americans are probably better in open space with field to run. That's just the way it's developed over time. However, what were seeing now with the indoor game, more and more Americans are starting to show how their skills are useful in the box game as well. Down the road, we're going to see some of this work together; the best teams are going to have American style and Canadian style players. There's always Canadians that play like Americans and Americans that play like Canadians. You look at a guy like Mark Steenhuis from Buffalo. He plays a lot like an American guy: running in space, using his footwork more than anything to create space and open opportunities. Then you've got some guys that are like a Curt Malawsky – the pure box guy. The ball is never in his stick. If it is, it's probably in the back of the goal a half second later. There are lots of different styles of players. I think ultimately, the sport has been around forever, but it hasn't been around at this level. More and more Canadians are going down to the U.S. and being successful in U.S. colleges; John Grant, Tracey Kelusky – guys that have dominant careers in college. We're starting to get a crossover. All those skills are going to mesh together, and I think it's going to product a better game and a better product."

Brad Banister admits that the league is made up primarily of Canadians.

"There's been a rivalry (between U.S. and Canadian players). Their field athletes are great conditioned athletes. Many of these guys went to Ivy League schools and take their lacrosse very seriously. They're very good at it. When you put them into a small arena, you can kind of manipulate your skills a little bit easier because you don't have as much room to run around."

Brad Berrow notices some American players have struggled with the defensive aspects to the game.

"You don't play the same way in field lacrosse. It doesn't matter if you're coaching box lacrosse or field lacrosse, everyone wants that same player, that tough player that can work, take a beating in a small confined area, and still be an offensive threat. There are not a lot of those guys to go around."

According to Kaleb Toth, a lot of Americans don't know how to take or give a hit because they don't play box lacrosse.

"They shy away from the middle because of that. But the one thing about the American players is they are all in great shape. They all can run like the wind and all have great skill. If they were to learn the box game, I think a lot of the good American players would be top box lacrosse players.

"It's one of those things you have to keep learning. From Canada, a lot of lacrosse players play hockey, so they know how to take a hit. In field, it's a more controlled game like soccer. It's not a big rough and tumble game. They always dominate us in field lacrosse, but we seem to dominate them in box. One day, the two worlds will come together."

Brad Banister: "When we opened up against Montreal and got our butts beat, we had 14,000 people in the building. Everybody was freaking out. I'm all nervous about the game, how we're going to do, etcetera, etcetera. There were a lot of expansion guys who couldn't make other teams that played for us. I'm sitting with Barry Black, who happened to be the GM of Everest. Our goalie at the time was questionable. I think we took the lead right away. There were a bunch of shots on our goalie. Barry Black is sitting behind me chewing gum, all excited, saying it's a good crowd, etcetera. You're going to do fine if your goalie is on. If he's not, you're going to suck. In the first five minutes, he's patting me on the shoulder and saying, 'He's on! He's on!' As soon as he said that, bang, bang, bang, we lost that game 7-16 and make a league record for goals against. That was opening night."

PART FIVE

LACROSSE
ONE STEP FARTHER

Chapter Nine:

Other Cups and Tournaments

Mann Cup

Canada's Senior Amateur Lacrosse Championship – the Mann Cup – is the lacrosse player's Holy Grail. It represents the winner between the Ontario Lacrosse Association versus the Western Lacrosse Association.

The first Mann Cup goes back to 1910, when Sir Donald Mann, the chief architect of the Canadian Northern Railway, donated the championship trophy. The first recipient was the Toronto Youngs.

Games were played under field lacrosse rules until 1935, when box lacrosse took over. The Mann Cup is one of the most valuable trophies in sport.

Like professional baseball, 90 percent of all NLL players play in the summer leagues. However, the same 90 percent don't get paid to play either.

Teammates on an NLL team might end up as adversaries on a summer league team.

Tracey Kelusky points out, "They still play the game full out, so they might end up hurting an NLL teammate."

"It's definitely a community where everybody knows everybody," adds Pat McCready. "But as soon as you put on another jersey, that kindness seems to fade away. You just don't hold any grudges. It's a game, and you do what you have to do to win.

"There's no money at all – probably enough just to cover your gas. Out in B.C., all the teams are really close to each other. In the east, there's a lot of traveling involved. It's a close community. Everybody knows everybody.

Kaleb Toth says the difference between the two leagues (NLL and summer lacrosse) is the roughness.

"You're allowed to dress more players in the summer leagues, so you're going to have more fights, a couple more injuries, with more guys playing and hitting you all the time. The winter game has always been a faster game because there are only ten teams. In the summer leagues, as good as teams can be, I don't think that any one team would be able to beat an NLL team. You get the best of the best playing in the NLL. Summer league is more of a minor system.

"You have to come out of junior. You get drafted like you do in the NLL. You try out for the team that drafted you. If you make it, you're on the roster. The only difference is there are a lot more players drafted. You can go to university and still play summer lacrosse, as long as the two don't conflict. There are only likely a half dozen guys in summer lacrosse that actually get paid. Everybody else just does it for the love of the game."

According to John Grant Sr., anybody who has played enough lacrosse will tell you there is nothing better than the Mann Cup.

"You did the bus trips and the sacrifices during the summer. The best of the east plays the best in the west in a seven-game series. It's unbelievable for most people to win or experience a Mann Cup. You'll talk to NLL guys, and that's what they want to win. That's not to say the NLL is not as good. The history of the Mann Cup, the importance of it – that's what kids aspire to win. It's more of a representation from your town, like the Western Hockey League. The toughness of those kids being able to travel by bus and go through the schedule they go through, it's like what we have here in Sudbury, Sault Ste Marie; it's a tougher schedule. The mental toughness; you have to be a tougher person to adjust to that type of lifestyle."

Minto Cup

The Minto Cup is Canada's junior amateur lacrosse championship trophy – the oldest in lacrosse since 1901 at the Junior A level. Games are between the Ontario Lacrosse Association and the British Columbia Lacrosse Association. The original trophy was donated by Lord Minto, Canada's Governor General, on May 31, 1901.

Other Trophies and Cups

President's Cup – national box championships – Senior B; first awarded in 1964

Founder's Cup – first awarded in 1972 to national box champs – Junior B

P.D. Ross Cup and Victory Trophy – two divisions of senior men's – first awarded in 1984

First Nations Trophy – Junior men's – first awarded in 1985

College

There are approximately 240 schools at Division I, II, III, and junior college with lacrosse programs, and approximately 400 colleges are home to non-varsity lacrosse.

The Men's Collegiate Lacrosse Association (MCLA) is a new organization of men's collegiate club teams with nine conferences. It began in 2006 to bring more attention to collegiate club lacrosse.

The governing structure resembles the NCAA with its eligibility rules, national polls, All-Americans, and a national tournament deciding the national champion from both Divisions A and B.

The idea came about after the 1994 Creole Bowl in New Orleans, featuring the champions of the Lone Star Alliance and the SouthEastern Lacrosse Conference. That game's success led to the desire for a true national championship for collegiate club lacrosse.

College club programs, while linked to varsity lacrosse, were operated by their own board of directors and organized their own national league (United States Intercollegiate Lacrosse Association). The first championship game under the new umbrella was in St. Louis in 1997.

In 1999, the Associates club teams voted to drop out of the USILA in 1999 to join the newly formed national governing body: U.S. Lacrosse, which took a lead role in administration and putting on the national championship tournament (which expanded to 12 teams in 1999 and 16 teams in 2000).

With the blessing of U.S. Lacrosse, the Men's Collegiate Lacrosse Association (MCLA) was formed in 2006 to better serve collegiate club lacrosse. You might say it is virtual varsity lacrosse. There is still representation on the U.S. Lacrosse board, but the organization conducts its own administration and championship. About 200 teams were involved in the 2007 season with expected growth in years to come. The league represents the fastest growing segment of college men's lacrosse. Teams featured are representative of some of America's most notable universities, such as Arizona State, University of Oregon, University of Georgia, Boston College, Texas A&M, Brigham Young University, and University of Florida.

Brad Berrow: "We'd get off the airplane after flying to Victoria or wherever, and we'd go find a swimming pool. One night, a couple of the guys ended up behind the Hyatt Hotel by the airport and there's one of them pulling off the tarp, climbing in buck-naked, having himself a good swim. We all join in. Along comes security. We went over to another place. Me and my buddy dropped our gear and went into this pool. All of a sudden, I'm swimming alone. I look up and see a bouncer charging with a baseball bat. I was just quick enough and young enough at that time to grab all my gear and run."

International

"One of my most exciting moments was I played with Team Canada in 2002. We were losing to the Americans. I forget the score exactly. We literally came back and tied them, went to overtime and lost in overtime. Just to come back. It was in John Hopkins. It was packed. It was on TV. I just remember talking to my friends after and said I've never ever been that excited in a game. It was just unreal."
Jamie Bowen

International lacrosse competition goes back to the 19th century when the Iroquois played a team from Canada.

In 1904, lacrosse became a full medal sport at the Olympic Summer Games in St. Louis. Three teams competed: two from Canada (of which one team was made up of Mohawk Indians) and one from the United States. The Shamrock Lacrosse Team of Winnipeg won the gold medal. The St. Louis Amateur Athletic Association took the silver, and the Mohawk Indians received the bronze.

In the 1908 Olympic Summer Games in London, two teams attended: Canada and Great Britain. Not one player on the Canadian roster had played on the 1904 team. Canada took the gold with Britain as the obvious silver. The game would be relegated to a demonstration sport in future Olympics.

Results for the 1928 Olympic Summer Games in Amsterdam are sketchy at best. What we do know is there were three teams, representing Canada, U.S. (from John Hopkins University), and Great Britain.

In the 1932 Los Angeles Olympic Summer Games, only Canada and the United States competed. Again, the U.S. team was from John Hopkins University. Neither team carried players from the 1928 roster. This time, the U.S. took the gold. Three games were played in front of nearly 75,000 people at the Los Angeles Memorial Coliseum.

The final year for lacrosse at the Olympic Summer Games was in 1948 in London. This time, Canada bowed out and teams were represented by the U.S. and Great Britain. There was only a single game played at Wembley Stadium, which resulted in a 5-5 tie.

The World Championship Field Lacrosse tournament was formulated in 1960. Canada won the initial tournament, but the U.S. has dominated ever since. It's a nine-day competition that is held every four years in July.

The International Lacrosse Federation was set up in 1974 as the governing body of men's lacrosse and to set ground rules for international competition. Its members include: Australia, Iroquois Nationals, Ireland, Wales, United States, Sweden, Hong Kong, Germany, South Korea, Scotland, Finland, New Zealand, England, Denmark, Netherlands, Japan, Czech, Canada, and Italy. There are also six affiliate members, such as Argentina and Tonga.

Melbourne, Australia hosted the first World Lacrosse Championship in 1974, then Manchester England hosted in 1978. In 1988, the first Under-19 tournament was held in Adelaide, Australia; and in 2003, the first joint championship event was held for the Under-19 to include the International Federation of Women's Lacrosse Association.

The first World Indoor Championships was held in 1980 as a non-sanctioned event with Canada winning. The tournament became sanctioned by the International Lacrosse Federation in 2003 and held its first seven-day tournament in Ontario. Six nations competed in the inaugural competition with another win by Canada.

Chris Hall coached the Calgary Roughnecks from its inaugural season until midway through the 2007 season. He played box with the Victoria Shamrocks for nine years.

"I played one year in the original professional league in 1975 in Boston then came back home. I was playing with the Shamrocks when I noticed Canada had won the world field lacrosse championships in 1978. I had never played the field

Chris Hall (photo by Cory Shannon)

game. I looked at that with interest. A couple guys – Don Hamilton and Bob Babcock in Vancouver – were organizing what was called a Canada West team. There had been no field lacrosse in British Columbia for decades. They were going to take this team down to a tournament at Stanford University in Palo Alto, California.

"A few of us from Victoria went over to the camp in Vancouver. The Canadian national team that had won the world championships in 1978, there was only about a couple of guys from the west that had been selected and hadn't been to the tryouts. Don Hamilton and Bob Babcock brought a bunch of sticks out. We were used to playing with wood sticks. They brought out aluminum-handled sticks with plastic heads. There were some that were six feet long and some that were short. They threw them out on the field and said, 'Go get a stick.' There must have been 100 players there. You knew there were only going to be 20 spots on the team. They all ran out and grabbed the short stick. Nobody wanted to grab a long one. I thought my odds would be a lot better if I picked up a big stick than a short one. I picked up a long poll; it was a defenseman's stick. I started to play defense."

Hall made the team and went to California for his first experience with international field lacrosse. He decided he wanted to form his own field team and organization and got together a couple of friends, found a sponsor, and started a team in Victoria. It won 76 straight games over five or six years then went back to the tournament in Stanford and won seven years in a row.

He also made the 1982 World Games national team and played in the world championships in Baltimore. In 1984, a world tournament linked to the Olympic Games in Los Angeles was called the Jim Thorpe Memorial Game. Hall made the All-World team. Then in 1986, he played on the national team at the World Games in Toronto.

Hall got the head coaching job for the national team. He went to the 1990 World Championships in Australia, then again in 1994 in England.

"Through that time, I became pretty connected with the lacrosse organizing bodies. I served on the International lacrosse Federation. We met annually to discuss competition and the growth of the game and what's going to happen with the game internationally. That was a great experience for me in developing the game worldwide.

"The United States has done a great job in growing the game. They were instrumental in developing the game in Japan. The world championships are now in Germany, Sweden, Czechoslovakia, Japan, Australia, and England. The game has really taken off and is growing worldwide. Being able to meet with those people and serve on those committees and help in some small way to grow the game has been a wonderful experience. Now, I think the bonus of that is we have friends around the globe. If you go and travel some place, there's lacrosse tournaments around the world that you can go to in all divisions: men, women, elite, master, and grand master. It's a real fraternity you can go anywhere on the planet and find people who are playing the game of lacrosse. It's going to grow further."

Kurt Silcott still thinks lacrosse would be a great Olympic Winter Game – box lacrosse.

"I think that would be great exposure for the sport. There's a group that's trying to head in that direction. The Olympic Committee and their rules state that a certain amount of countries have to play. I know we're not there yet. Once you make it an Olympic sport, there are a lot of countries out there – they want to compete in an Olympic sport. If it's not an Olympic sport, they don't care. You've got countries like Australia, England, and Scotland – they're all playing lacrosse. They're all playing some version – field or some modified version of the two. If you set up rules and have games like the Heritage Games, you'd get more membership. It's just another one of those things where we're not quite there yet. The great thing about the Olympics is they are every four years. If it came in as a trial sport, four years later, there would be countries that would put teams together. I saw a Japanese team play a field game in Baltimore years ago. Sure, they're not at the level of the Americans or Canadians, but they can play lacrosse. Women's hockey is a great example. When you put it out there, people start playing. If you did the same thing with lacrosse, a lot of countries would call upon Canadian and U.S. coaches to come over and teach the sport."

Luke Gilbert: "We went bowling – just a team bonding thing. We lined up like dodge ball, like back in seventh grade. You picked the most athletic kid first and the worst kid last. We all lined up and had the five captains up front to pick teams. Everyone was teasing before we even did it that whoever was last, no one respects them; they're the worst athlete. If you can't bowl, then you're pretty un-athletic. There is this big juggling – who's going to be last? Sure enough, I was the last one. I found out later it was planned. It was pretty humiliating. I was talking a good game and had been one of the new guys that had stepped it up. Then all of a sudden get picked last."

Chapter Ten:

Growth and Development

Grassroots

There are a lot of events that play into developing minor lacrosse. Organizations are more organized today. There is parity of sport at the Division 1 level. Sport clinics give kids a first-hand opportunity to try it out. Indoor facilities are increasing, somewhat.

But perhaps the best example for promoting growth at the grassroots level is having a strong professional league. Notwithstanding, televising that professional league goes a long way to building that foundation.

When the 2005 All Star Game and Champion's Cup Final aired on CNBC Europe and CNBC Asia networks, it had the potential of reaching a combined 50 million homes throughout Europe and Asia. That not only helps expose the game domestically, but internationally.

NBC carried the above 2005 games live across U.S. – making it the first live network broadcast for the sport of lacrosse. A game of the week package aired on America One affiliated stations (117) and regional sports networks, including Cox Sports Television, C-SET, Charlotte-based TV network of the NBA Charlotte Bobcats. OLN, which was later named Versus, and the NLL struck a partnership for the 2007 season where Saturday night telecasts aired.

All of this has a huge impact for the growth of the game.

Goalie Anthony Cosmo started playing lacrosse when he was about nine years old. The opportunities for youth lacrosse are much greater today than when Cosmo held his first stick.

"When I started, it wasn't something to pursue or anything. It was something to take up my time while I was playing hockey. The minor programs are blooming everywhere in every city. The opportunity for kids to come to this level (NLL) is also there. The minor leagues are improving, and that means our game is improving."

When a kid can turn on the television and see lacrosse a game that he plays is being played by pros, it makes a

difference. Kurt Silcott says it shows there is another place to continue the sport when he turns 21.

"It's a goal to reach for. Kids turn on TV, and they see lacrosse. That's what they want to play. If you never see that pro league anywhere, you think after 'this' year, my dream is done. It ends."

It's hard to explain the hold that lacrosse has had on players. Brad MacDonald began playing at age four.

"I come from a really small town. Lacrosse was all there was to do. My dad got me started early. I played a little hockey, a little baseball, but lacrosse I couldn't give up. It's honestly addicting. People you talk to, who would see their first game, wouldn't miss another one."

Kevin Dostie describes himself as a pick and roll guy. With a degree in business, he started lacrosse much later in Windsor at age 14.

"I just had a bunch of hockey friends tell me, 'Listen, we're playing lacrosse. Soccer is kind of a sissy sport.' I kind of got tired playing soccer, so I started playing lacrosse and fell in love with it."

Jamey Bowen saw his neighbor play in the 1976 Commonwealth Games in Edmonton, where lacrosse was a demonstration sport. Bowen was playing soccer at the time.

"I didn't know what the heck it was (lacrosse). I was seven. I went the next year (to play lacrosse). The following year, I got two more buddies in from hockey. Literally, the third year was almost a complete transformation of the hockey team to lacrosse just for hand-eye and fitness. In high school, I had a hockey scholarship and a lacrosse scholarship. I picked lacrosse."

Regarding grassroots opportunities in Edmonton, Bowen admits he wasn't aware of any.

"That was the big drop off. I think maybe I'm here because of attrition. Everybody else dropped to the side. I still enjoyed it and got my schooling through it. Now, I'm a high school teacher and run a lacrosse academy. Even though maybe financially, the lacrosse game hasn't done anything, it's definitely opened some doors for camps and other stuff. Since then, with the pro game, it gives kids a chance to shoot for something…scholarships. You can talk to the Wray boys (Taylor and Devan). They got $100,000 to go to Duke. It's big business now. It's real owners with real money and NHL guys behind them and NHL arenas, and NHL-sized fans. It's really evolved."

John Tavares was introduced to the game in downtown Toronto.

"My older brother Danny played for a lacrosse program for kids, to keep them out of trouble. We had an outdoor lacrosse box hockey rink during the summer. I'd always take my brother's stick and go to the box to play at age four or five. I've played ever since."

Brad Banister grew up in Calgary where the only opportunity was scrumming with a bunch of kids at an outdoor rink.

"We were playing against guys, when we were 14 and 15 years old that were 20 and older. We were kind of self-taught, self-coached, self-financed to go to the Founders Cup or what else. Now you can see 3,200 strong with a 30 percent increase in enrollment every year. There are coaching clinics all over the place and no lack of lacrosse opportunities in Calgary right now."

Ten years ago in Okotoks, a town just south of Calgary, Alberta, Banister was going for a jog with a lacrosse stick in hand. "An older gal pulled me over and said there was talk of this program starting up. Would you get involved in it? I did. We had about 17 kids of mixed ages. They were hockey players in the winter who wanted to be lacrosse players in the summer. I went with that for a year, then stopped. In another three or four years, I fired it up again. This time, we went from 48 players to 400 registered in three or four years. For the parents, we have a drop-in shinny; it's called the Masters League. It's really caught on.

"You drive through Calgary, Okotoks, Airdrie, Cochrane, wherever, now you can see kids walk down the street with lacrosse sticks. I think about once a week I get a call from a dad telling me, thanks for getting his kid involved in lacrosse. He's got to put another window in his barn or garage or basement.

"A lot of the rinks in Calgary are sand-based, cement, or concrete. That causes a big problem in the summer when the ice comes out. You can't play on sand under boards. Every place is short of buildings right now. Even when the Roughnecks are in town, we can't even find a place to practice. We're definitely in a demand for rinks. It's hard to find a place to play. You can go out on the grass to play, but it's not really the same game. But, it's coming. They're building new rinks all the time. There are almost 4,000 people playing in this area alone. When I was growing up, there were maybe 14 of us."

Devan Wray started playing lacrosse when he was 12 years old in Edmonton. He went to Junior A with the Burnaby Lakers before heading to Duke University for college lacrosse. "When I was growing up, there was very little opportunity, or at least, it was untapped opportunity. The biggest opportunity was going down to the U.S. on a lacrosse scholarship. When I started playing lacrosse, even when I was in the junior ranks, I didn't really think there was a future in the professional level. I never thought I'd be stepping on the floor at the Air Canada Center or the Pengrowth Saddledome, Pepsi Center, Rexall Place in front of 10,000 – 15,000 fans, especially growing up in Alberta. Every time I step on the floor at the Saddledome, it's something special. I grew up watching the Flames and the Oilers battle in hockey. In Edmonton, I remember sitting in the stands cheering my brains out for the Oilers and thinking how great it would be to be in that position. We're not making hockey-type dollars, but I get to step out on the floor in front of thousands of fans.

"The pro level impacts lower levels absolutely, especially in a province like Alberta. In B.C., the lower mainland and Vancouver Island are huge for lacrosse. Out east and in southern Ontario, there is lacrosse everywhere. In Alberta, lacrosse at the minor level has only just started to take off. The presence of the Roughnecks just opens up thousands of more parents' and kids' eyes to what a great sport

Photo by Cory Shannon

it is. It takes years, but eventually that will trickle up. You've got more kids playing at a young age, more teams where they can go, and more talented lacrosse players coming up. Eventually that will lead to a stronger National Lacrosse League."

If grassroots lacrosse is more developed in British Columbia, it's because the weather is a lot better year-round than in Alberta. Kids can play outside and in outdoor rinks. The nice thing about the summer box lacrosse is you don't have to pay for the ice machine or the freezing plant.

"With lacrosse, you basically learn how to catch and throw," says Banister. "Everybody can walk, run, stop, and turn. You're on the heels of your feet all the time. It's not as bad going into the corners as hockey. You have your balance. You don't have to worry about the six-foot three kid coming after the five-foot eight kid. You're planted and ready to go."

Luke Gilbert grew up in Baltimore, Maryland and experienced having around 5,000 fans watching some of his Division 1 games in college. "It is pretty much the hotbed of outdoor lacrosse. I started when I was in eighth grade. I was much better at playing basketball. I thought I was going to college for basketball. I kind of got into the whole recruiting process for lacrosse. They just saw athletic ability over a lacrosse player but wanted to make me into a better lacrosse player.

"Once you play high school, it's who's athletic and who can finish. Once you get into college, it's a lot more structured. That's where you learn what your role is. That's consistent with indoor and outdoor. We have a groundball guy, a face-off guy, the guy who loves the body and holds his play inside and rough people up. Everyone really has a role. That gets set in college."

If you talk to most of the American-born players, even though box lacrosse is played in the pros and college, the outdoor game will always be first, maybe because it started from the grassroots level.

"I still love playing outdoor," says Gilbert. "That's my favorite. Outdoor is amazing. I play with the Marin Lacrosse Club. They're the best in the West. They go to Hawaii, Lake Tahoe, Portland, and all over the country – just a group of guys that were Division 1 All-Americans. They still want to play, but they don't want the commitment playing professional. It's just a blast. You sack it up and play hard for two games then you go on the beach or wherever. You get a lot better, but at the same time, it's a lot more relaxed. Kind of like the street ball to basketball. You throw different moves and stick tricks that you wouldn't do normally. It's a lot of fun, and you get to play with a lot of good players that you wouldn't have been able to in college or junior."

The NLL actively supports grassroots lacrosse.

"We work with all the provincial and U.S. lacrosse associations with different initiatives," reports Jim Jennings. "We donate a lot of money to a lot of youth organizations. Our best effort for junior lacrosse and youth lacrosse is just doing more of what we're doing now – getting on network television and letting organizations build off of that."

The Growth of the Game

Brad Berrow saw a lot of opportunities in the sport for both growth and learning. He remembers a day when they had to make their own pads.

"Sticks cost $3. As a kid, you don't think about it. You just can't wait to play. I think I was lucky because I was on a wave where there were a lot of kids playing with talent that were teaching the game, so you learned it. It wasn't work, even though you worked really hard at it. You were given the opportunity to try different things so you could use your own initiative and creativity."

One of Berrow's role models includes goalie Don Hamilton. He was fascinated the way he played the game. He went to games and watched different goalies to see and learn how they did different things.

"I didn't watch it so much for pleasure but from a technical aspect. Another guy close to my own age – Dave Evans – when I was 14 or 15, he was already in Junior A and went on to play for Vancouver and Montreal in the old pro league. Eventually, I ended up playing with him in Vancouver. And although I couldn't play at his level, I certainly learned a ton of things, so it was fun."

When Berrow started playing, after the minor levels at the time, you might possibly go to Junior B, Junior A, then perhaps Senior B or Senior A.

"Of course, there was the old inner city league or the Western Lacrosse Association. That was the epitome of lacrosse at that point. Two years before I got out of junior, there was an old pro league, then it collapsed. For five months, they were going to pay you $6,000 back in the early 1970s. If you had a job and a family, which a lot of guys did, they didn't go play, so it wasn't necessarily the best lacrosse. Then everybody came back to the

WLA. When I got up there, it still had the professional mentality, so we worked real hard and took it serious."

The WLA has similar rules to the NLL now.

"You used to have screen or mesh around the back, but the side boards were open," says Berrow. "You were right next to the action. It really brought the game close in. Some of the guys' padding was taped and held together, especially goalies. There's a look to an old-style lacrosse goalie. He's got gear that's taped and hanging off him, homemade stuff, but they looked capable. Now the styles are very generic. In the old days, you had a lot of different styles and different type of equipment."

Casey Powell hails from northern New York, and like most Americans, grew up playing field lacrosse.

"The sport is certainly growing for sure. Fans are more aware of it on a national basis and throughout North America. We're looked upon as being more professional. People look at us as hockey player-style professionals. In telling people I play lacrosse, they used to go, oh, is that semi-pro? Is that a club team? We'd always have to correct and tell them, no, it's professional. Now, more people are aware of it."

Having the professional or bigger-than-life role models has helped impact the growth of the game. The Gait twins, Gary and Paul put themselves on the map in 1988. They had a profound impact on the game. It was their stick skills and athleticism that mesmerized audiences – especially the Air Gait move that originated in the box. What happened was Gary charged from the rear of the goal. He would then suddenly jump clear over the cage and appear to almost hang suspended in mid-air and simultaneously fire a shot past the goalie, landing in the crease.

"We idolized Gary Gait and Paul Gait," adds Powell. "They went to Syracuse. Our first game was in 1988, and we watched Gary Gait play for Syracuse. We fell in love with him and his brother's style of play. We just wanted to be those guys from the day we saw their first game."

Jim Moss recognizes that regardless of where you were born or where you end up, there is always an opportunity to make a difference and carry a lacrosse stick. He grew up in Ontario and had only lived in California for 18 months at the end of the 2005 NLL season when he started building a lacrosse network throughout the state through coaching lacrosse clinics and camps, plus volunteering with the Stanford women's team.

"The lacrosse community here has been so good to me. They just opened their arms to embrace me. Moving to California has allowed me to make lacrosse a full-time life. In return, I will give everything I have back to California lacrosse to bring it up to the same level as the rest of the country and in North America so that the kids here can compete. The day I see a kid that grew up in San Jose playing for the San Jose Stealth, I'll feel like my work has paid off."

A sure-fire way to measure growth is by looking at the NLL and expansion. In 2005, the league welcomed two new teams: Portland and Edmonton. In 2007, it was Chicago. In 2008 – Boston.

"It's great for the league," says Kaleb Toth. "It brings out national exposure, Canadian exposure, and ultimately the States. It makes the league that more credible."

Jamey Bowen was involved in trying to bring a pro team to Edmonton a few years ago. It didn't happen.

"Finally, when Bruce Urban stepped up and made everything happen, it just snowballed from there. The media has been great. The community has been great. It gives some of the Edmonton guys a chance. Three quarters of our team got tryouts because of the team. Even if they tried out and got cut, they got that chance to do that."

Jamey Bowen: "The goal I scored (at the start of the 2005 season) – the first one that will go into the books as long as these franchises are around. And to have my little guy there was really special. He's four. I did a quote in the paper and I gave him the game ball. He said, 'Daddy, I'd rather have gum.' The next day, I got about five packages of gum from other people who said they would take the ball."

Chapter Eleven:

Conclusion – For the Love of the Game

Anthony Cosmo

"You can't describe it. Being on the floor is something incredible for a lacrosse player because this was never one of our dreams. Growing up, it was playing in a major league – a senior league. We never thought of it as being a pro league to play in. It's an experience that hopefully my kids, my children's children, and more get to experience.

"People who play lacrosse, we're all at the same level. We do the same things. We try to be in the community and promote our sport as much as possible. We try to be as personable as possible. This opportunity is incredible. We can't let it go to waste. Kids ask for autographs and for help here and there, we have to go out of our way to do it. I think that will help us promote our sport.

"Everybody has friends and even best friends on the opposite teams. It's fun playing against them, although, on the floor, they're your enemy. Afterwards, it's good to sit back and talk."

"We go as long as we can. Most of the players are playing because we love it. We grew up loving the sport. Guys aren't out here for the money. Although the money is available, we've never seen the money before. Until our bodies say no, we're going. Of most of the guys who retire, it's not the mind that is retiring; it's the body."

Brad MacDonald

"It's a pretty passionate game. There are a lot of family ties in it. With the guys on our team, it feels like a family.

"Walking into the arena with the fans, it's the adrenalin. To play in front of 15,000 – 19,000 people, it's huge. It's hard to describe. It's numbing to be there.

"Before you come here, you know what a team thing is – but then you go on the road trips, you go on the three-hour plane ride, go to the hotel, and get to spend every minute of every day for three days with these guys. I can talk to this guy; he's got three kids, a wife for 10 years, and he's almost as old as my dad. You know what? He's just down to earth. He's willing to help me out. It's pretty neat. You learn a lot of stuff from the older guys. I hope when I get to that age, I can help the young guys like they helped me."

Kevin Dostie

"The passion comes like with any other sport, with the glory. Everyone wants to win. The hard-hitting, action-packed game, that's what keeps us playing. Everyone wants to be a winner. With no passion, you're never going to be a winner. You've got to love the game.

"There's the adrenalin of being out there. It doesn't have anything to do with the fans. It's just the game, one-on-one combat, pick and rolls, everything about it."

Luke Gilbert

"My brother was the one that kept me going with it. He played defense, and I played offense out in the back yard. We had battles. We didn't have any neighbors so we had to be best friends. We had to play with one another. He kept me playing lacrosse even though I never really wanted to.

"Then I went to my first college, had two years playing Division 1 and got burnt out. I wanted to give it up. I hated lacrosse. I met Doug Locker (Assistant General Manager, San Jose Stealth), came out to the west coast and thoroughly rejuvenated. I love lacrosse. I love being on the west coast."

Kaleb Toth

"The onc thing I've always said about lacrosse players is we take every game personal. We try 100 percent in everything we do. Although we do have a lot of fun out there, you're not going to see any high sticks or anything like that or a hit from behind. It's going to get intense, and we want to win. We pride ourselves on our sport. We love our sport, and the only way to showcase it is to play hard every single night.

"Sports, in general, teaches you a lot – how to work as a team. It teaches you a lot about respect: respect your coaches, officials, and basically the game. I've been very fortunate in lacrosse and hockey where it has opened up a lot of doors for me in the business world and the friend world. If it wasn't for sports, I don't know where I'd be. I'm sure I wouldn't be as happy as I am now. It's taught me a lot about life, how to grow up, and do what you need to do in this world to compete."

Jim Moss

"Loyalty, intensity, and passion, those three words sum it up perfectly. The best part about being a professional lacrosse player, you have all the things you have in the rest of your life, but I don't think there is anything I'll be as passionate about as I am with lacrosse. I'm not going to find a job selling widgets, where I'm going to be that passionate about widgets. I'm passionate about lacrosse. I'm fortunate that it's sprung up into other jobs in this sport. I don't know if I would have found anything that I was that passionate about."

Brad Berrow

"When I first got involved, I moved to the lower mainland in British Columbia, the first time I saw it, I was fascinated with it. It occupied all my time from when I was 10 until I was 23. I did nothing but go to the box every day, play and work on my stick, work on my skills. I'd play with anybody just because I loved it. I couldn't get enough of it.

"It's almost like it's a cult following. It has so many elements. It has a lot of violence in it and aggression. It challenges you to be very physically fit. You can't glide. There are no stoppages; you've got to go.

"I don't know how to describe it except it was something that I thought about all the time. School was something around it. My whole life, my whole social life was organized around this thing. You'd go to school, come home, grab the stick and goalie pads. I walked a mile and a half to go to the lacrosse box, put on the equipment, and wait for people to show up. If they didn't show up, I'd run around the rink with my pads and practice throwing because I had to anyway. You wear all your gear when you play. It seemed that someone would know that a goalie was at the box, and they'd show up anyway.

"I'd play with little kids. It didn't matter what age I was. From when I was playing with Vancouver or lower levels, I'd go to the box and put my gear on, I'd have kids from tyke or six, up to guys my own age. They'd come to a practice and try different things to make a guy better.

"I never considered myself to have any God-given talent, but I worked like hell. I was prepared to sacrifice my body and pay for it."

Kyle Goundrey

"The fact we have other jobs and do this shows the passion we have for the game. This isn't our life. We're not making millions of dollars. In some cases, we're sacrificing pay, sacrificing family, sacrificing a lot to play the game we love. No matter what anyone gets paid, it comes down to the passion of the game.

"Everybody is a professional, but when you're on the floor, you're playing with the passion of the game or there wouldn't be a game. You can't go out and say, I can't do this because I'm a professional. I think the reason that professional sports are successful is that professionalism is taken off the floor and you are just the best player at that sport. The passion you have for the game is what drives the game."

Damien Davis

"It's fun. The competition is great – to get out and run around, a lot of contact, a lot of good guys to play with and play against. I don't think I have too many enemies in the league. After the games, everyone goes for cold beers."

Lewis Ratcliff

"Lacrosse is one of the most important things in my life. Behind family, it's probably number two. I don't know anybody who plays lacrosse that doesn't absolutely love it. This isn't a job. It's what you'd be doing for free anyway.

"I think it's more a family type of aspect where not everyone is going to get along all the time, but you know they're always going to be there for you when you need them. The boys are going to have your back on the floor. Everybody is there for the same goal. Everyone is trying to obtain the same thing. It's basically just like a family. Everyone is looking out for everybody."

Taylor Wray

"A lot of the guys have played junior lacrosse together, grew up playing together, or played against each other for a number of years. Everybody has a familiarity. There's just sort of a common bond between lacrosse players. They're very similar personality types. I haven't been on too many teams where guys haven't meshed together.

"I actually live in Charlotte, North Carolina. I go to graduate school there and coach in Division II lacrosse at Queens University of Charlotte. I fly back for the game. It takes a little bit out of me, but when you look forward to every weekend as much as I do, it doesn't seem like much to fly."

John Grant Sr.

"It taught me mental toughness. I grew up with a big old trunk, a hand-me-down – my brother played. Every lacrosse season, I had to use his pads – the old felt pads. You take your hockey gear and put it in the trunk and pull out the lacrosse gear, sew the stuffing back into the pads, and away you go. You grew up at the rink. There was that inner toughness. You have one pair of running shoes in the summer and one pair of rubber boots in the winter. We'd hop fences, play cowboys and Indians, and lacrosse all day. It's a sport that you create. You don't need a whole lot of people around you. You can go to a wall. I tell kids the Gary Gait story, how every day, he'd go to the school and shoot balls and develop a skill. You create things with backyard lacrosse. John (Grant Jr.) and Tracey (Kelusky) grew up together and played. When I was playing, they'd go to the rink. They'd be on the floor after practice and after the game. Everywhere they went, they had their stick in their hand. It builds your confidence. Whatever age or level you participate at, you learn from it."

Jamey Bowen

"With lacrosse, you mention a nickname, everybody knows him, be it from Peterborough, Victoria, or Kalamazoo. It's a good group of people."

Kurt Silcott

"I've dealt with athletes my whole life. I've played sports my whole life. There is a passion in lacrosse that I don't think is matched in any other sport. I think it comes from a few different things. One, it's the game. The game is a little different than most games. It's got a little bit of every sport out there – a piece of that in lacrosse: hand-eye coordination, put the ball at the end of your stick, footwork, and the athleticism. There is also a bond amongst lacrosse players that is different from other sports. You're sitting somewhere chatting with someone in a restaurant and find out that person played lacrosse, there's an instant bond, whether they've played in Canada or the U.S. or wherever. It's an interesting game that way."

Casey Powell

"I live in Newport Beach. The more I look at it, the more I can't believe that people fly across North America for a home game, then have to go back to work as soon as they get home on Monday morning. Some of the guys might take a Sunday shift. They do it for the passion. It's certainly not the money. It's the camaraderie of being a professional lacrosse player.

"It's in our blood. It's something we've been doing for a long time. It's really opened doors for us. My father worked in a paper mill. My mother was a secretary at our school, and they never played sports. Myself and my two younger brothers got full scholarships to Syracuse because of the sport, and now we play it professionally. We get to travel around the world. It's opened doors and changed our family. What it's done for us, and the feeling we get when we walk in a stadium, it's not just about playing. It's about being on the bus trip with your buddies, in the locker room, and just being around the game and the aura of it. It's something special. I think a lot of the Native American roots had a lot to do with it – the spirituality of the game. This is one of the very few sports, at the end of the game, you can fight a guy and then you'd be drinking a beer with him afterwards. We're a brotherhood."

BIBLIOGRAPHY

American Sport Education Program. Coaching Youth Lacrosse. Human Kinetics, 1997

Busby, Ian. Sports. FFWD, November 1, 2001

Down, John. Roughnecks' fireplug about to get his chance. Calgary Herald, December 6, 2004

Hinkson, Jim. Lacrosse Fundamentals. Warwick Publishing, 1993, 2000

Hinkson, Jim. Lacrosse Team Strategies. Warwick Publishing, 1996

Hinkson, Jim; Jiloty, John; Carpenter, Robert. Lacrosse for Dummies. John Wiley & Sons Canada Ltd., 2003

Morris, Daniel. The Confident Coach's Guild to Teaching Lacrosse. The Lyons Press, 2005

National Lacrosse Hall of Fame, William Maddren U.S. Lacrosse, Inc., 2005

Pietramala, David G. and Grauer, Neil A. Lacrosse Technique & Tradition. John Hopkins University Press, Baltimore, 2006

The Birth of Modern North American Lacrosse 1850-1900. E-Lacrosse.com

Pilson, Ty. Don't quit your day jobs: Roughnecks are 'regular guys' just working for the weekend. Calgary Sun, February 8, 2005

Pilson, Ty. Goal frozen in time. Calgary Sun, May 2, 2004

Schmeisser, William C. U.S. Lacrosse, www.uslacrosse.org

Smith, Theresa. Moss makes Jim-dandy deal. The Denver Post, 2/13/07

Stevens, Neil. NLL tweaks its rules. NLL Press, 12/29/0

TSN Staff. Mammoth acquire Moss from Stealth, 2/7/07, www.tsn.ca

Vennum Jr., Thomas. American Indian Lacrosse. Little Brother of War. Smithsonian Institution Press, 1994

Wolff, Alexander. Get the stick. Sports Illustrated, April 25, 2005

www.adanaclacrosse.com
www.calgaryroughnecks.com
www.collegelax.us
www.cstv.com
www.e-lacrosse.com
www.fogolax.com
www.insidelacrosse.com
www.intlaxfed.org: International Lacrosse Federation
www.lacrosse.ca
www.lax.com
www.laxbooks.com
www.laxpower.com
www.mcla.us
www.mll.com
www.nll.com
www.plpa.com
www.sportsnet.ca -- Ben Knight
www.uslacrosse.com
www.usssportscamps.com
www.worldindoorlacrosse.com

ABOUT THE AUTHOR

Debbie Elicksen

- Authored, edited, and project managed over 50 books for both royalty and self-publishers
- National Hockey League and professional sports reporter for over 12 years

Photo by Lawrence Chrismas

- Author and Publisher of

  Inside the NHL Dream (A behind the scenes look at the NHL, ISBN 978-0-9730237-0-1)

  Positive Sports: Professional athletes and mentoring youth (ISBN 978-0-9730237-3-2)

  Future Prospects (A behind the scenes look at major junior hockey, ISBN 978-0-9730237-4-9)

  Creating a Legacy: The Calgary Booster Club (The Calgary Booster Club was the catalyst for bringing Calgary the 1988 Olympic Winter Games, ISBN 978-0-9730237-2-5)

  Loyalty, Intensity, and Passion (A behind the scenes look at the National Lacrosse League, ISBN 978-0-9730237-5-6)

  Inside the Canadian Football League (ISBN 0-9730237-6-3; scheduled for publication 2008)

- Author of Self-Publishing 101 (Self-Counsel Press; ISBN 1-55180-639-8)
- Publish a monthly e-newsletter Inside Publishing
- Teach Book Publishing 101 and Manuscripts Made Easy workshops
- Keynote speaker
- Appeared on Vicki Gabereau (CTV) and the NHL Network
- Independent Publishers Association of Canada Vice President
- Served on the City of Calgary Sports Policy Steering Committee
- First woman to headman a football conference in Canada (President of the Prairie Football Conference)
- Public Relations Director for Edmonton Trappers Baseball Club, working closely with the California Angels
- Calgary 1988 Olympic Winter Games, Hockey Committee, Media Liaison
- Canadian Junior Football League, Director of Public Relations and Marketing
- Calgary Colts Junior Football Club, President, Assistant General Manager
- Mentor with Alberta Mentor Foundation
- Member of Alberta's Promise (for initiatives championing youth)

WE CAN HELP YOUR BOOK COME TRUE

Freelance Communications provides publishing support to authors, self-publishers, and companies that produce books to market their business, including annual reports. We help those who are time-stressed, have a passion for an idea, and want to leave a positive impact. Debbie Elicksen has authored, edited, and project-managed over 50 books for both royalty and self-publishers. People come to us for the following services:

- Writing and editing
- Full project management
- Graphic design and layout
- ISBN and National Library Cataloguing (in Canada)
- Marketing and distribution planning and support
- Printing

Our job is to produce a professional looking, well-edited product that would be welcome in any bookstore or retail counter plus make the process as seamless as possible and keep the author from panicking and hyperventilating when they think it's becoming all so overwhelming.

If you have any more questions, please feel free to call or email. We look forward to the possibility of working with people who have an inspiring message.

Contact Debbie Elicksen
Freelance Communications
(403) 240-1340
delicksen@shaw.ca
www.freelancepublishing.net

LOYALTY, INTENSITY, AND PASSION
AN INSIDE LOOK AT THE NATIONAL LACROSSE LEAGUE

Sports
2007
Softcover, $15.00
ISBN 978-09730237-5-6
5.25" x 8.25"
Black and white photos
Rights held: world, English
www.freelancepublishing.net

Loyalty, Intensity, and Passion takes a behind the scenes look into the world of professional lacrosse. This book looks at some of its unique aspects. More than just a game, lacrosse is a way of life.

Games are hard-hitting, action-packed, and full of atmosphere. The play could be described as similar to basketball with pick and rolls with inside and outside shots. However the rough and ready contact is more like hockey.

Players take a personal responsibility for selling the game to the fans. They know if the game grows, so do the opportunities. Many of these players have other jobs and careers and commute from extreme distances to play. Even though they are professionals, they play lacrosse simply for the love of the game. Most players are new to the business side and prefer to negotiate their own contracts rather than hire an agent. Money is not their incentive to play.

Loyalty, Intensity, and Passion exposes the true essence of the game, how it has grown throughout North America over the past number of years, and where its future lies. The reader is left with a strong inside knowledge of what it's like to be a player, the challenges faced, the life-long camaraderie, and perhaps reinforce their own feelings about the sport.

BOOK ORDERING INFORMATION

Order online by credit card at www.freelancepublishing.net or make check or money order payable to:

Freelance Communications
#45, 3809 – 45 Street SW
Calgary, Alberta, Canada
T3E 3H4

$15.00 (Please include shipping/handling $3 CDN/$5 USD)

► Bulk rates available (i.e. teams, development camps, etc.)
► Personalized printings available for orders of 500 or more of one title

GST registration # 89426 436